Accepting Unconditional Love

Ruth Cherry, Ph.D.

Copyright © 2021 by Ruth Cherry, Ph.D.

All rights reserved. No part of this publication may be reproduced, distributed, or transmitted in any form or by any means, including photocopying, recording, or other electronic or mechanical methods, without the prior written permission of the publisher, except in the case brief quotations embodied in critical reviews and other noncommercial uses permitted by copyright law.

ISBN: 978-1-63945-229-3 (Paperback)
       978-1-63945-230-9 (Ebook)

The views expressed in this book are solely those of the author and do not necessarily reflect the views of the publisher, and the publisher hereby disclaims any responsibility for them.

Writers' Branding
1800-608-6550
www.writersbranding.com
orders@writersbranding.com

Contents

Introduction v
Part One vii

Chapter One 1
Chapter Two 7
Chapter Three 13
Chapter Four 17
Chapter Five 21
Chapter Six 23
Chapter Seven 25
Chapter Eight 29
Chapter Nine 31
Chapter Ten 35
Chapter Eleven 41
Chapter Twelve 45
Chapter Thirteen 47
Chapter Fourteen 49
Chapter Fifteen 53
Chapter Sixteen 57
Chapter Seventeen 59
Chapter Eighteen 65
Chapter Nineteen 71
Chapter Twenty 75
Chapter Twenty One 79
Chapter Twenty Two 83

Chapter Twenty Three 85
Chapter Twenty Four 89
Chapter Twenty Five 93
Chapter Twenty Six 95
Chapter Twenty Seven 99
Chapter Twenty Eight 101
Chapter Twenty Nine 103
Chapter Thirty 105
Chapter Thirty One 109
Chapter Thirty Two 113
Chapter Thirty Three 115

Part Two 121

Introduction

In more than forty years practicing individual psychotherapy I have experienced being human in various dimensions of comfort, joy, disappointment, rage, sadness, betrayal, surprise, excitement, grief, and delight. I have walked with hundreds of others in their process of discovering depths in themselves they hadn't known. As we humans live with attention and commitment, our lives become sacred playgrounds.

I have learned about the immense power of our inner worlds in creating our outer world encounters. Our unspoken thoughts, feelings, beliefs, and expectations come back to us as we notice our reflection in others' words and acts. The seamless fabric of our life experience, inner and outer, proves to be precisely and personally meaningful.

I have marveled at the creativity of humans who don't accept limitations. Our faith and trust carry us when our intellects and our strong backs can't. I have witnessed unexplained healing in meditation. It seems magical that we humans can access a power greater than our own. I notice Source (God, Spirit, Infinite Intelligence, All-That-Is, Universe, Essence) reaching out to us every second, more available to us than we know, always pulling us to greater plateaus of well-being and self-expression.

Against this rich background of appreciation for an intricately designed, benevolent, wise world I have been given the wonderful opportunity to experience my personal healing of Multiple Sclerosis. With all that I have learned and experienced, I embrace this challenge. The gift of this diagnosis tells me that I am supported and trusted. With intuitive guidance I chart my course. My meditations illumine my path.

I invite you to accompany me on this journey to pave a path, reliable and trustworthy, that you can use to integrate your life experiences. You will find yourself in these pages. Enjoy the unmapped possibilities of your ever-expanding journey.

PART ONE

Chapter One

Our challenge is to accept Source's unconditional love for us. Not to earn it. We are already worthy and we can do nothing to make ourselves more worthy. Yes, we are flawed and sometimes we don't use good judgment. Nevertheless, Source loves us absolutely and without limit.

Acknowledging this reality can be rough when we are used to efforting and struggling and feeling disappointed and always settling for less than we really want. After all, learning our role and performing it gives us boundaries and focus and makes our expectations "realistic." Accepting reality, however, clouds our perceptions of Source. Source is unlimited. We cannot employ logic or reason to know Source. Our intellects prove to be irrelevant. Can I have everything I want? Source shouts **Yes**. Our friends say, "Well, maybe not everything. Be realistic. Don't expect too much."

However, Source says, **Yes** and **Come on** and **Let's go**. Source passionately and enthusiastically responds to our dreams and always supports us. **Source is unfailingly on our side**. And Source cannot be hoodwinked. Source loves us completely but Source also knows that we don't love ourselves. Sometimes we overeat or we work compulsively or we silence our feelings instead of speaking. When we deny our integrity, Source loves us anyway but Source also insists that we love ourselves.

And we so resist accepting and loving ourselves.

Better to be not-quite-ready-but-working-on-it. Certainly, when you stay busy folks around you take you seriously. I imagine that Source laughs. We chase our tails and exhaust ourselves and lose sleep. For what?

Only for our Controller to (maybe) nod approvingly. We confuse doing and being and we confuse our Controller with Source. We each have a Controller who tells us what is expected and appropriate. That's all it does. It doesn't love us. The Controller may dole out a few gold stars intermittently but they fade too soon and don't seem sufficient for the effort we invest. In about ten minutes another project presents itself and our intellects race off in several directions, bustling activity offering us a distraction. A distraction from our experience of presence. Presence to ourselves, in this second. And that's all. Being and not doing (temporarily) terrifies us. Thinking diverts our attention from our uncomfortable experience.

We love our intellects. They make us feel important. They may impress others. And they save us from truly experiencing what it is to be ourselves in the moment. What a deal! We give up our spontaneity and our desires and our dreams in exchange for a manufactured safety which isn't safe or comfortable or really what we want. We'd rather not be all of who we are. We prefer to live a diminished life.

We won't accept restrictions of our movement — we go where we want when we want. We demand respect from others in their speech and behavior towards us. But we don't treat ourselves respectfully. We act like we don't value our feelings. In fact, we're proud of not "giving in" to our needs. We fear that our inner worlds slow us down instead of realizing that our inner worlds lead us to our unlimitedness.

At our core, the deepest place in us, the place where we're most ourselves, we are expressions of Source Energy.

Notice what your intellect says about that! And then notice your thoughts without thinking your thoughts. Watch the antics of your mind as though you are viewing cartoon characters. Identify with a passive Observer standing behind a window. Watch your thoughts and feelings on the other side of the window. Practicing detachment in this way lends perspective. And perspective allows us to transcend our limited thinking. When we transcend our limited thinking, we question our willingness to accept a small life — health-wise, financially, relationship-wise, creatively.

The truth is we don't need to settle.

Settling is a way of cutting off our feelings. "If I don't want too much, I won't be disappointed." That's never true, though. If we don't want to be too much ourselves we may keep others comfortable but what damage do we inflict upon our souls? And how can we allow ourselves to damage our own vitality?

We have a responsibility to live large — to know what we feel, to acknowledge our inner world, and to accept ourselves. Each of us is unique. We each have a particular gift to offer the world; no one else can deliver our gift.

Source needs us to be ourselves fully. To do so requires that we accept Source's unconditional love for us. And that demands attention and clarity.

When I first awaken, I linger in bed, checking in with Source. I'm open, questioning what is today about? And then I listen. I don't hear words but I receive a feeling or an attitude or a perspective. I want to see as Source sees. I move into a receiver position and I notice. My Controller only activates when I arise so, for these few quiet minutes in the dark, I simply notice.

This morning I envisioned a Source light at my center. The light burns with perfect health. Source wants me to be perfectly healthy and knows how to create perfect health in my body. Today the doctors may point to brain lesions on an MRI and give me a label. That, however, is irrelevant to Source who knows no limitation. And when I am one with the light at my center, I know as Source knows.

That kind of knowing isn't intellectual. It's entirely intuitive and depends upon my openness and my availability to receive. I love that it doesn't require work or energy or a strong back. Availability is the only criterion. Is my heart open? Am I paying attention to this second? Am I available for healing?

Healing is knowing as Source knows. Healing doesn't require specialized information but self-discipline helps us to access our own truth. The light at my center shines. I need to check in with it and experience this clarity. Self-discipline focuses my attention inward. That's all. I don't have to learn another fact or conquer a bad habit or achieve a goal. What exists this second is the perfect platform for me to heal. I start from right here, right now. I am in the right place this second.

I close all the doors to my past. My childhood wasn't comfortable, friendships didn't work out well, I've made some serious errors in judgment. But so what? Today none of that matters. In fact, today none of that exists unless I resuscitate the memories. But when I choose healing I lock the doors to the past. I say, "Thank you for today just the way it is." I acknowledge my partnership with Source who always pulls me to healing. I can cooperate with my own healing or I can resist.

Why would any of us resist cooperating with Source?

Because it feels scary and unpredictable and totally vulnerable. Some of us have had unpleasant to traumatic experiences when we were vulnerable to powerful others in our younger days. But now we choose to live in the present. We're not walking down well-trod paths one more time. Now we're partnering with Source and we let Source show us the path.

We invite Source to heal us and we pay attention. We don't think. Our Controller, anchored in our intellect, will talk us out of this completely unrealistic stance. But then our Controller doesn't truly believe that healing is possible. Our Controller is earthbound. Its point of reference is totally intellectual and external. Our Controller knows what someone else has done before us and uses that to limit our expectations for what we can do for ourselves. Our Controller is a fine part of us which we use when we maintain our cars or balance our checkbooks or clean our homes. But our Controller hasn't much to offer when we choose healing.

And healing is a choice. "If it's that easy," you may say, "everyone would choose healing."

Healing is a choice but it's not easy. It demands vigilance. We want to know: What vibration am I practicing this second? Do I truly want to practice that vibration or is another vibration more conducive to healing?

Healing demands a constant reference to our inner world, not allowing our vision to be influenced by the outer world. We don't pay attention when another tells us, "You can't do that. No one else has, so why do you think you can?" With our attention firmly anchored in our Source Energy center, we trust our guidance completely. Our trust is based on experience paying attention to our inner world tugs. We take action only when inspired to do so. We trust our own experience more than we trust knowledge that another has shared.

We view our experience as sacred. Our experience evolves momentarily and is completely our own. No one else has lived our life before us and no one ever will. We are not here to "do life right" or to meet someone's expectations. We are not here to clean up the world's messes or to impress anyone or to earn acclaim. We live and we notice and we pay attention. And always we stay present to ourselves, acknowledging that at our deepest center Source dwells.

Trusting that fact focuses our attention. When we need or fear or hurt or want, we move into our deepest center. We don't chase shiny distractions — fame or wealth or achievement — when we want to experience peace. We move into our center and we allow peace for peace already exists there. This second in your deepest center, Source is. We choose stillness and we check in and always we say Yes.

Sometimes when we are still and we check in, we feel old emotional wounds. We may choose physical healing but Source doesn't discriminate. If old wounds still live inside us, Source knows. And Source will guide us in our healing on every level. We are one person — physically, emotionally, mentally, spiritually. If anything lives unhealed today in any part of us, Source will direct us to our healing in that and every other part of us. We focus on the present second and notice *what is* this second.

Source knows us completely and knows us in our perfect health. Source focuses upon our health, not our lack of health. So, while our quirks and distortions exist as a result of mistaken beliefs, Source knows us in our wholeness. And loves us unconditionally.

A mistaken belief most of us share is that we are limited. Either we believe that we are limited by accidents of birth — gender, geography, physical situation, or intellectual acuity — or we believe we are limited because we blame someone else for not being what we wanted.

The mistaken belief that we are limited can be used to assuage our fear that we are not good enough, another mistaken belief. "What if I try and give my best shot and still I can't make my life work?" "What if I am not acceptable to other folks?" "What if, no matter how much I want my life's dream, I can't make it happen?" Better to not want than to be disappointed.

But that's so nuts!!!!

Why wouldn't we want the very best for ourselves? Why wouldn't we want everything? Rather than choosing limitation, we say, "Yes, I am here and I count!"

That confidence and optimism arise only from our anchor in our Source Energy center. <u>Only</u> from our Source Energy center. Only when we sense, then experience, then know, then trust Source's unconditional love for us can we hope to allow healing on a magnificent level. **Healing is experiencing our oneness with Source**. Then experiencing that oneness again and again. Then allowing Source to guide us.

Only Source knows what perfect healing looks like for each one of us. All we can do is practice presence, practice trust, and allow. Source directs us. And, hopefully, we cooperate.

Why wouldn't we cooperate?

Chapter Two

In a meditation last year, I realized that I had written a book. For seven months I had kept journaling notes about my challenges walking, my application of Universal wisdom principles to my every day experience, and my growing awareness of myself as a participant in a larger flow. I had written articles for years about psychology, spirituality, and meditation. Following my meditation insight I consolidated all these pages and watched **Living in the Flow: Practicing Vibrational Alignment** appear.

I love that book because it didn't feel like work. I don't feel proprietary about the content. I let words come as I played at taking dictation while I sat at my computer. I had no notion that what I was writing would emerge as a book. I simply enjoyed the effortless experience in the moment of watching the words and sentences materialize on the screen in front of me. I appreciated my role as totally passive receiver. I didn't have a goal, I wasn't struggling, and I wasn't concerned with an outcome. I allowed a process my intellect didn't choose and I watched.

Creating is allowing. Healing is allowing. In both I pay attention but I'm clear that I don't initiate the flow.

I focused on behavior in the first half of life — doing, thinking, struggling, accomplishing. **But now in the second half of life I'm more concerned with allowing a wisdom greater than my mind's to lead me**. I can't see the path to get to where I want to go from where I stand and yet I know there is a path and I know that it is available to me. I also know that I will see it step by step, day by day.

I'm very clear that I can do nothing significant about my healing on my own. What I want is beyond anything I've done or anyone else has done. I want a miracle. I want to walk perfectly for as long as I choose. And I want to feel peace.

The latter may be the more challenging desire but I suspect that it forms the foundation for receiving everything else that I want. Being grounded in peace and living from that deepest eternal center in me precedes the manifestation of the details. What is to doubt when I'm anchored in my Source Energy center?

I felt that clarity while compiling the articles for **Living in the Flow: Practicing Vibrational Alignment**. I knew I was healing and I trusted that I would heal completely. When I finished the journal writing for the book, I was walking or swimming a mile a day. I loved being active and I felt victorious.

But shortly thereafter my body changed in surprising and unwanted ways. I stopped swimming due to shoulder aches. I had pushed through the pain for as long as I could, further damaging my shoulders. My Controller operates as a relentless taskmaster who doesn't tolerate slacking. I hurt myself physically through my Controller's strong will to perform. When I couldn't swim I clung to the side of the pool, kicking and jumping. Finally, after several weeks I reluctantly acknowledged that even this activity weakened me. My Controller was so sure that exercise was the path to healing that I didn't notice or question that assumption.

When I discontinued water exercise, I vowed to walk. I would walk every day, two times a day. I would set a distance goal and stick to it. And, yes, it took me many weeks to acknowledge that walking exhausted me and I wasn't recovering. I drove my body as hard as I could. The Controller striving attitude that had served me well in the past now damaged me. I didn't want to accept that.

After months of exhaustion and discouragement, I surrendered. What else could I do? I certainly had tried everything active until I felt sure that nothing I could <u>do</u> served me in my healing. Not a truth I came to easily or joyfully.

Historically, I've practiced a frustration vibration intensely without knowing that I was doing so, a result of my Controller dominance in the first half of life. I was doing what I had been taught was right. I thought that if I did everything well, I would gain what I wanted. It didn't work perfectly but I didn't admit it. No matter how diligently I strove, love didn't appear as I had hoped. I didn't feel valued and appreciated. I committed decades to achieving, however. My Controller didn't allow me to feel the disappointment and the sadness and the loneliness. I just kept pushing.

With time and age that had to stop. At mid-life I moved into my feelings and let them crash over me. My inner world took prominence. Living with that anchor inside has opened doors I hadn't seen and I've loved the last few years. I thought I had gotten IT and waited for my improved walking to illustrate that fact. So, when my walking became more challenging rather than easier, I was reluctant to acknowledge it. Until I couldn't not see it. I was shown in a client what I refused to see in myself.

I knew Source was present in my afternoon psychotherapy session. I pray when I'm with this client. He has been consistently resistant and controlling. I confronted him. His voice raised and his temper flared. After several minutes he moved into his fears and his frustrations and his feelings of being overwhelmed. Finally, he cried. It was a beautiful healing experience and I gave all the credit to Source.

My client's surrender showed me my need to surrender.

These days when I can't exercise I still see myself walking perfectly someday. Each step I take is good form but I can't walk as far as I'd like. My days of walking or swimming a mile are past. I had thought I was doing so well. I expected healing to follow an uncomplicated trajectory with steady improvements.

At this point healing has moved out of the behavioral realm into the vibrational realm. Since I can't physically do as much as I want, I focus on consciousness. I have said for decades that consciousness is the basis for health. Now my consciousness is all I can work with.

I have offered a daily guided meditation group for over a year. I felt inspired to do so and it has proven to be powerfully enlightening for me. Now an acquaintance who has received a devastating diagnosis has approached me. We meditate together forty-five minutes earlier in the day.

I love when Source brings opportunities to me. Immediately when Maggie and I spoke, the path showed itself. It wasn't a thought or a good idea, it was an inspiration. An inspiration feels undeniable. No thinking required. As a light turns on, the path appears.

Having prayed for guidance in my own healing, I am very grateful when Source responds with a definite suggestion. I jumped at the opportunity to partner with Source in this endeavor. Also, I felt excited that Maggie and I can work with Source and heal in a way for each of us that hasn't been clearly demonstrated before. Wouldn't it be fun to allow a miracle and to watch its manifestation?

Meditating 45 minutes twice a day now, I feel calmer and more trusting. Anxious thoughts don't bombard me and I don't pursue action. I feel heard and protected and watched over. Clearly, Source knows *what is* with me.

I have wished some things in the world would happen but no one is responding to me as I had hoped. Clearly, I am the constant. If everyone else is behaving in the same way towards me, I must be the one setting the tone. Apparently, I'm practicing a vibration that isn't supporting what I say I want.

So, I choose to practice the vibration of already-having, not the vibration of struggling-to-get. I choose to feel happy and gratified and worthy and both appreciative and appreciated. I choose to know that I have a place in the world and that I'm seen and known and valued. This is not a familiar vibration for me but I can assume it and trust it and know it until I see evidence manifesting. It must manifest at some point if I practice this vibration exclusively. I won't wobble or doubt. I know the truth of my healing and I'm waiting to see it. I don't need reassurance from others. I know my perfect health right now. That's all that matters today. That's how I participate in my own healing.

I'm realizing that this phase of healing is about complete surrender and trust. If I want physical healing I need to allow psychological and spiritual healing of my old distorted psychodynamics. I let go of what I've unconsciously assumed to be true to <u>allow</u> healing on a deeper level. I can't <u>do</u> anything to effect healing. I can practice vibrational alignment in my Source Energy center, I can monitor my thoughts and feelings, and I can use good judgment where that applies. But I've moved into a realm where I can't do anything in behavioral terms to effect healing. Now I choose to focus on my surrendered-and-trusting vibrational practice and I allow Source to heal me.

Trusting that I will be taken care of has not been a large part of my experience this lifetime. But now I must practice that unfamiliar attitude. All I can say is "OK, Source. I know my good comes to me now. Thanks." I'll wait and pay attention and be grateful for the little improvements. I do notice I'm standing straighter. I appreciate that.

I choose to enjoy each day in this process as I will enjoy each day when I'm walking well. My healing is real in vibrational terms today. The manifestation will follow. Now I'm in Source's arena. I can only allow. Quite a challenge for me but I'm ready and available. And truly happy to be in this process.

Chapter Three

Source is.

We can align with Source, practicing a Source Energy vibration or we can focus on ourselves. We each have a story. We can wrap ourselves up in the drama of it all or we can focus on our timeless Essence.

By the second half of life we've told our story too many times. In our own heads we have unwittingly adopted a role and identified with it. Now growth demands that we move into our Essence and live from there. That's the only stance that allows us to expand.

Moving into Essence and allowing proves to be totally without boundaries. We often say, "We are all one." Usually we mean that all individuals share a common core. Another understanding is that within ourselves we are one person expressing in several dimensions — physical, psychological, mental, and spiritual. Health covers every dimension. Only the individual knows what is honest and what is distorted within him/herself. We can't judge another. We can only know ourselves in depth. And that knowing isn't intellectual. Very little about moving into health is intellectual.

Health lies more with allowing than with trying. We bypass our thoughts and memories and identify with our eternal core. Being carries us where doing can't. Surrender is the only stance that allows healing and surrender requires humility. That implies feeling our fear, recognizing our confusion, and owning our cluelessness about restoring our health.

Simple behavioral changes our intellects can manage. Healing is deeper than behavior, though. You can do everything right and still not be a healthy version of yourself. You can impress others and garner acclaim but if you are cut off from your Source Energy core, it's all show.

Being open to health requires stillness. We can't stay overly busy and engaged with the outer world and maintain an anchor in our Source Energy core. At least not all the time. We humans so fear stillness. We love it when another person pays attention to us and fully receives us by practicing presence. But we resist practicing presence for ourselves.

It's like we want to relate to ourselves as others have related to us. We adopt an orientation and treat ourselves the way a certain frame of thought directs us. We may say, "I'm a Buddhist and I know this lifetime is a solitary journey so I don't pay attention to my loneliness. I can transcend that aspect of being human." Or we think, "I will be so successful as a health care professional that no one can question my worth. Yes, I am exhausted but I take good care of my clients." Or we make meditation an ordeal rather than an experience. We talk about the length of time we meditate rather than focusing on simply paying attention. We move into our head (our Controller) and ignore our heart.

Experience is our path to our deepest Source Energy center. Focusing on any minute's particular experience isn't the end but it shows us the way. It's the process that counts, not any specific content. We pay attention to early childhood abuse not to remain stuck in that experience but to notice it and to allow ourselves to be carried beyond it. We don't move beyond our wounds through denial nor by holding on to our powerless role. We practice presence and we allow healing.

The spiritual flow which is always available to us carries us when we open to our experience. Psychologically, this truth has been documented for decades. I want to expand this hypothesis to the physical realm. Referring only to my own experience of physical health or lack of well-being, I want to test the hypothesis that my hanging out in my Source Energy center will heal me physically. I want to participate in the unlimitedness that is Source. I know I can't experience it by thinking. So, I will be still and pay attention and surrender and trust. And know my own truth that at my core I am healthy.

Source is. I am one with Source. That's all I need to know.

Chapter Four

I love feeling unlimited. Of course, thinking guarantees that I can't access my unlimited core. But that core is there all the time. Source is always available to me but I'm not always available to Source. I say that I choose to always be available but the right words don't necessarily imply a receptive heart.

Receptivity is key. I don't need to be good enough for Source; I only need to be open and available.

How can we always be receptive to healing? What does it take to maintain a receptive stance?

Always a stream of well-being flows to us and through us. Being receptive means trusting the stream and allowing the stream to carry us. We don't know what is best for us but we know that the stream does, so we practice trust and allowing. When we receive an inspiration, we act on it. We don't use good judgment or think about the consequences. We say "Yes" and we jump. But only when we're inspired. Until then we practice stillness.

Part of this process is knowing a truth which isn't visible or reasonable. Knowing isn't believing or hoping.

We know we are worthy and we always trust that. Our Controller tells us that we are not worthy and not to risk vulnerability. But experience is not in the Controller's realm. We dismiss the Controller and don't listen to its words in the realm of being. We embrace our vulnerability and we anchor in vulnerability and trust. We take a risk. We speak and allow ourselves to be known (if that is our challenge) or stay silent (if that is our challenge). We don't choose out of habit. We don't play it safe. And we don't worry.

Being receptive every second is living with passion. We turn away from our limited thinking and our fears and we accept *whatever is* in the second. We allow gifts to rain on us. We expect gifts and we practice gratitude in advance. Not being open scares us more than being disappointed. We learn that openness implies allowing and allowing will carry us through everything. We don't fear our feelings or another's disapproval. We choose to be available.

After the second meditation group today I trusted this attitude. My friend Karen came and meditated with me. She sings professionally, a locally recognized artist. She inspires me with her joy and her readiness to participate. She's not self-conscious and she's always ready to laugh. Playfully, we have considered cooperatively writing blues tunes — she writes the music, I write the words. So as not to incur our Controllers' judgments, we have specified that our tunes will be really bad. I had written a long, truly awful song which was great fun to write. At the end of our meditation today I glimpsed an image of Karen singing it with her duo buddy.

I felt reluctant to share my imagery with Karen. It seemed so silly. But I want to receive Source's unconditional love so I ignored my Controller's warning. I described my imagery to Karen. This choice proved pivotal. In this tiny way I said Yes to Source and No to my Controller. This opened me to receive Source's love. When I play it safe and act appropriately I'm relating to my Controller. When I spark in response to an image or an intuition, I accept Source's invitation to dance.

I so want to heal physically and I know Source is my only hope. Of course, I will accept any overture from Source. This tiny example is insignificant in content but life-changing in my attitude. I want to heal. I must partner with Source to allow healing.

Allowing Source in my days attunes me to the tiniest details. No one would know if I disregarded this slight tug. But the energy and aliveness I experienced after I mentioned it felt like barbed wire falling away from my lower back. I moved without as much constriction. I lifted my right leg more easily.

I look for these tiny indications of healing. I notice correlations which I generally wouldn't see but I am so focused on accepting Source's unconditional love as my path to healing that I want to be aware of details.

I choose to partner with Source in this healing endeavor so I want to notice Source reaching out to me. Source is aware of me every second and knows precisely what I'm thinking and feeling. Source knows me better than I know myself. Experiencing that so powerfully in the second during meditation blows me away. Source wants me to heal as much as I want to heal. Source shows me the path but the path doesn't present itself in a way I expect. It doesn't even make sense that sharing my silly image leads to physical healing for me.

Except that it does.

In the grandest of schemes, reality is momentary and vibrational. I change my vibration on one level and notice consequences on another. I risked being silly and loosened the constraints on my spontaneity. Some constraints on my physical movement lifted immediately. This healing I experienced in the moment.

It only makes sense to me. My consciousness is my playing field. No one else really knows my inner world landscape. But that is the personally specific context for my healing.

The diagnosis given to me is the same as the diagnosis given to many others. However, what it means to me is completely individual as far as my own consciousness distortions and my own opportunities to heal those distortions.

In our powerless days we saw ourselves and the world from a perspective different from how we experience ourselves when we know we are powerful expressions of Source Energy. Of course, my power comes from allowing Source to move in my life. I identify with my eternal Essence and I watch. I stay out of the way and I enjoy being led.

Over my years practicing as a psychotherapist, folks have questioned how I could listen to clients complain. That always surprises me because my experience of therapy is that the client and I dance with Source. Source leads us and we pay attention and follow Source's guidance. Then we notice what comes from the outer world. So psychotherapy becomes an opportunity for the client to learn how to notice Source, how to receive Source, and how to trust Source. We terminate therapy when the client feels solid in interpreting and processing her experience.

How does anyone move through life without meaningfully appreciating her experience?

Every day and every second Source beckons to us. Our Controller distracts us so that we can't feel Source reaching out to us but always Source reaches in our direction. We remember that when we can't feel it. We know that Source always pulls us to healing but we don't know what healing looks like. We rely on our trust for Source's love for us. We know reality is far greater than our Controller intellect grasps. We maintain an attitude of optimism and confidence and allowing.

Source is our foundation.

Chapter Five

Sunday I felt Source's support powerfully. I gave the talk at a Unity church a few miles away. In the afternoon I offered a two-hour workshop. The miracle for me lay in trusting that I would be led.

Historically, I have avoided public speaking. When I spoke I felt self-conscious and self-critical. I expected others to be critical of me, also. And, surely, I received what I expected. Thus, allowing myself to be known scared me. I preferred withdrawal and invisibility.

The last few years have offered many opportunities to experience inclusion, however. I have released my anxiety as I have received increasing acceptance from myself and from others. I'm revising my expectation of public speaking to anticipate joy. Looking forward to the Sunday work day, I felt light-hearted. I had offered the talk previously so I wasn't concerned about that. When I tried to prepare the workshop material, however, I felt blocked. I trusted Source to guide me.

Everything worked well. My physical energy during the day proved to be more than adequate. I was <u>on</u> for several hours and I practiced presence and allowed Source to lead. We all had fun and considered new ways of being. I found the day to be delightful. I drove home, very grateful and very satisfied. I felt so much energy running through me that I couldn't sleep easily that night but I had no complaints.

Partnering with Source pulls back curtains. I notice Source in tiny comments and details. I feel patient and I speak easily and trustingly because I'm focused on allowing. Whatever I do becomes an opportunity to observe Source in action. What's better than that?

I expect miracles and I expect support and I expect gifts. And then I open to receive them.

Meditating facilitates receiving. I get out of my way and I create a space and I watch. I practice allowing.

The big gift I'm open to receive is perfect health and great walking. What I experienced Sunday is that Source supports me in the moment. Thinking blocks my receiving from Source but practicing presence allows Source. On Sunday I did fine with my presenting. I felt healed in the moment when I interacted with the group. As an introvert, I find this amusing. What I have feared has morphed into my salvation.

So, I expect that healing my walking will happen in the moment as I'm present and as I allow. Exactly the opposite of moving into my Controller who schemes and works to press forward. **Healing comes from partnering with the Universe and allowing**. I need to pay attention. The Universe offers me signs which I can't receive them when I'm in my Controller, thinking. I need to be completely humble, available, and, yes, happy about this mutual project.

Honestly, I do trust that Source supports me and supports everything I want and, maybe, more. I want to choose joy in every moment of this journey. Eventually, as my walking continues to improve, I will be overwhelmingly happy. I'll practice that joy today.

Interesting that the little jumps in progress come from interpersonal events and not from working at walking. Progress walking comes from opening my heart, from realizing that it is safe to do so now, from enjoying my experience on this earth plane. The more I meditate and immerse myself in the non-physical, the more I enjoy being in the physical. The fewer the struggles and the doubts inside me, the more fun my experience with others is. And, apparently, the more I heal. Physical healing follows emotional healing.

Chapter Six

Accepting Source's unconditional love for me baffles me. Why would I not accept love?

In meditation today I noticed how much my subtle thoughts reflect unhappy memories. Many times I didn't speak up for myself. Many more times I've used poor judgment. I've practiced my share of self-destructive behaviors over decades. But in meditation I looked at my thoughts about the past and realized that thinking about the past keeps me from experiencing the present moment. The content of the thoughts doesn't matter. **This moment is fine and this moment is also the only place I can experience Source**.

Why would I not choose to always be present?

Actually, I don't care why. When I notice how much I lose by not paying attention to this moment, I loudly proclaim, "Never again! Never again will I wallow in that decades old muck. Never again will I resurrect anger for folks long gone. Never again will I avoid living my life today." I am destroying myself in ways no one else can. I am hurting myself more than anyone ever has. I have let myself get caught in old misery, keeping it alive.

What an idiot I've been! Of course, I can't accept Source's love when I'm not present. Any tugs at my attention, especially tugs carrying me back to a powerless, frustrating time, absolutely close my availability to Source. I can be present to Source, open and available to receive gifts and healing or I can refight battles I've already lost. I can prolong my frustration or I can close that door to the past. But apparently I have to close the door repeatedly for it keeps sliding open.

Today is better than any day in the past. The possibility of healing mightily in the future beckons. What's to question? I don't care what has happened. No matter what, I can't foreclose on today's opportunity. Source asks me today, **Want to receive my unconditional love? Or would you prefer to practice resentment?** It's my choice; Source will accept whatever I choose.

I choose to release resentment, to practice forgiveness, and to look to the future. And I need to re-choose every second. When I catch myself somewhere other than right here, I'll pull myself up and turn myself around. No justification, no apology. Just a steady commitment to being present each second. That's work and it works. That's how I practice being available to receive Source's unconditional love.

And that's how my body will continue healing.

Immediately upon making the decision to release the past, my walking improved a bit. I did some errands easily and quickly. Strangers smiled. I felt carried in the flow. When I do my inside work, the outside reflects a greater ease. So confirming. That's what working with the Universe feels like. I don't push or try to control or take action. I can't force what I want to happen but I can trust the Universe, allow it to carry me, and pay attention to my guidance. That's how healing happens.

It's one thought at a time. Oops, that thought wandered back to childhood. OK, be present here now. Two seconds later another oops. And thirty seconds later another. That's OK. I'll pull myself into the present as frequently as I need.

Chapter Seven

For what happens to us, we are responsible. For encounters with strangers, we are responsible. Depending upon the depth with which we choose to live, we can recognize that life shows us ourselves and shows us our path. If we'd prefer to be clueless, we can. If we want to notice our consciousness in the tiniest detail inside us and around us, we'll appreciate the perfect mirror of our inner world that the outer world offers.

Others say the words we've only thought. We can accept that illustration as instruction for ourselves or we can make others wrong. One way of demeaning others is to help them. That's also a way of refusing to look at ourselves.

We are here to do our own work — to practice humility, to embrace our vulnerability, to surrender, and to trust. In the second half of life we get no gold stars for achievement. Availability is the only consideration. We receive what we need and want when we practice presence and we pay attention. No effort is required.

Why do we resist knowing our inner worlds? **Our inner worlds form the basis for everything we experience in the outer world**. If I'm angry with myself, I'll (unconsciously) rope in another person to act that out for me. She's just showing me myself when I don't pay attention to what's happening inside. I don't make the incident interpersonal. I accept it as a message from my inner world. Always I look inside when something outside ruffles my feelings.

Our inner worlds can be challenging to know. Definitely, we want to learn the patterns of our unconscious dynamics. And we can.

First, we decide that it's necessary to know ourselves in depth. We release our attachment to seeing ourselves as "nice" and "helpful." We accept that a power we can't imagine flows to us and through us. We cannot be proprietary about our experience.

We move into the Observer behind the Observer window and we notice *whatever is*, without judgment or criticism. We practice being. Simply being. We choose humility. Reality is grander than our intellects can grasp. We open to notice this reality. We don't take anything personally and we stay on our own side. We renounce victimhood and blaming.

We acknowledge our Shadows and we commit to healing the parts of our inner world that scare us. We have everything inside us and some of it we hope others don't notice. But we want to notice whatever exists in us. We are vibrant, evolving beings. Nothing in us dooms us permanently. Our self-hatred and our self-sabotage and our confusion and our hopelessness are real. As adults we allow healing. We show up every day, we practice presence, and we watch as Source directs our attention.

Source always pulls us to heal. Source wants the very best for us. Source doesn't harbor anger for us and Source never withdraws from us. Source shows us how to grow out of our childhood perceptions and beliefs. We may, however, choose to identify with our fears and limit ourselves rather than move into our expanded self.

Why would we do that? Why do we hesitate to receive from Source?

The deal Source offers us is better than receiving a million dollars from a stranger. All we need to do is pay attention and allow. And we'll receive precise guidance every step of the way. We don't have to come up with a life plan. We don't have to do anything. Mostly we need to not do.

So, Source says, **I'll show you what will bring you immense joy**. **Trust me.** And we choke. Clearly, we don't trust Source. Apparently, we'd rather live partly closed down lives, with the illusion that we're in control. We resist living with passion. We choose less instead of more. Whose side are we on?

We have a human center where our human subpersonalities anchor. From there we take care of business with its mundane specifics. Hopefully, we use good judgment.

Beyond the human level lies our eternal center. In our human center we learn skills which others have perfected. In our eternal center we trust our own particular inspiration. We live to experience and, thus, to grow. Whatever happens offers an intriguing adventure. Possibility beckons. We don't know the outcome or even the path but we're up for the experience. Living with passion means saying Yes when a door opens to us.

What does the experience of saying Yes to Source's love look like and feel like?

Some passivity in order to receive seems necessary. Definitely there can be no striving. We open to receive what already exists. It's impersonal in the sense that it reflects Source. And, yet, intensely personal in that Source knows us better than anyone else could know us and better than we know ourselves. Source absolutely believes in us. Knowing our past and our foibles and our immaturity and our tunnel vision, still Source is our biggest supporter. Source knows possibilities for us that we can't imagine. Source doesn't limit us. Source knows what others have done but can see more for us if we choose more.

I choose more!

Source's love for me will heal me completely. I know that and I trust that and I enjoy watching it happen.

Chapter Eight

Accepting unconditional love. I've never had that experience. I don't know what to do.

That's just it — there is nothing for me to do. My shoulders drop a little as I let go. I breathe. I don't look around because what is around me doesn't matter. I stay inside myself. I focus on this second. This second is all there is. It's a perfect second. I didn't create it but I can enjoy it and appreciate it. Thanks for this second.

I have a place in the Universe and I count. That fact already exists. I can't enhance it or diminish it. I can accept it. Source accepts me. With everything Source knows and can do, Source values me.

Source needs me to expand itself. I can offer a unique perspective which has never existed before and never will again. And I am enough.

Chapter Nine

The Universe knows everything you want and the Universe is arranging events to bring you your dream. Don't fight it. Life has meaning and order. Pay attention and work with life.

If you were vibrating at the equivalent frequency to what you say you want, you'd have it now. So, apparently you need to practice a new vibration. Life will show you how. Notice your experience and learn from it. We have the most wonderful teacher in life. All of your lessons are about aligning your Source Energy center (You) and your human center (you).

We are both physical and non-physical. It's easy to identify with our physical self. But our physical self can't lead us to healing, to transformation, and to joy. Those come from allowing our non-physical center to guide us. We expand as we move into our Observer and allow.

We know we create our own experience. Let's create with awareness, not by default. **The vibrational frequency we practice draws encounters and experiences in the world to us**. We are not only observers of *what is*, we create *what is*. Let's take responsibility for that truth. "Yes, I create my experience. Yes, I am responsible for everything that happens to me."

We notice what happens to us. We notice how the world impacts us. We notice folks around us and we know that they show us our inner world. We know that our inner world is all we need be concerned with. For if we are in balance inside us, the outer world will reflect that balance.

The outside reflects the inside. We can't point fingers at anyone else. We can only say, "Thank you for showing me myself." We are here to learn and we can always learn something more. We never finish. The Universe always supports us and guides us in our growth. Its lessons may be subtle but they are consistent.

It all comes down to our choice to practice resistance or to release resistance. Our two centers, physical and non-physical, have integrated when life flows smoothly for us. When we resist our non-physical center, we feel frustrated.

Why would we resist?

Some things we can control and some things we can't. Trusting what we can't control may scare us until we anchor solidly in our eternal center. In meditation we learn to know our inner world. It's landscape is as sure as the landscape around us. But sometimes we don't want to acknowledge it.

We fuel our anger when our inner world beckons and we don't go with it. Our anger hides our fear. We are not in control of the direction of our growth. Whether our lesson is assertion or humility or stillness or action, we can't resist it and feel content. If we have an agenda, we'll try to pound life into the form we prefer. When we realize that we can't, we need to sit back, trust, and allow life to guide us.

Why not? After years being ourselves, we know well the limits of our competence. We know that Source is unlimited. We know that Source supports us in being everything we want. We also know that Source guides us. All we need do is open to all of ourselves.

We spend time in silence, we pay attention to our inner world experience. We notice our outer world experience. We know that the outer world mirrors our inner world. We welcome our guidance. Every day we are ready to learn.

Anchoring in our eternal center changes our experience of ourselves and of others. The tenor of our days shifts slightly. We notice Source where we haven't before. We realize Source has always been available to us but we haven't seen that or wanted to know that. Using judgment from our Controller intellect in our physical center, we have squeezed ourselves off from Source. We thought we were keeping ourselves safe. But safety has no place when we choose expansion and integration and transformation.

How much of yourself do you want to embrace?

Source respects your answer whatever it is. Let's know consciously what answer we choose, not what we utter in words but how we live our days. We choose all the time. When we feel our feelings, we embrace ourselves. When we block our feelings and think exhaustively, we avoid ourselves.

Source is always present. Do we rely upon our Source guidance? By mid-life we know that we don't have all the answers. Do we stop asking the questions? Do we settle for a "pretty good" life? Do we convince ourselves that we're satisfied?

Can you practice stillness for an extended period?

Can you notice *what is* both inside you and around you and practice acceptance in the moment?

Can you say Yes to your inner world experience without reacting to conditions?

Can you dream big?

Can you allow yourself to want what hasn't existed before and truly know that it's possible for you?

Chapter Ten

I'm greedy.

I want more and more. And I want bigger and bigger.

More and more and more and more. And bigger and bigger and bigger and BIGGER.

I don't accept that I can't have it all. I don't accept that I can't have what no one else has ever had. Why accept limitation, especially before I've asked?

I know I can't have everything I want by trying. I know it only comes through experiencing Source. I know I can't have everything I want by impressing Source. I know that the only way I can have everything is by allowing my Source Energy center influence to grow. I want to give it more time and reverent attention. That's where my version of Source power lies. Practicing vibrational alignment with Source offers me opportunities I can't imagine in my human center. In my eternal center, I am unlimited.

There's nothing to do. I want to maintain a receptive momentum, not deviating from my Source Energy center vibration.

But I do deviate many, many times every day. OK, that's how it is being human. I am completely human but I am also divine. I want to practice blending all that I am. I don't want to fret and I don't want to float, at least not all the time. Mostly, I want to live in awareness of my oneness with Source.

I want to always remember that I am loved, loved more than I can love. I am loved more than I've ever experienced being loved by a human. I am loved without end and without condition. I can't imagine that kind of love. I've never seen it and certainly never felt it from anyone else.

When I allow that love to flow through me I experience an immense love for life, for being, for *what is*. It's love for this second just the way it is. It's love for anyone I meet just as they are in the second. It's absolute acceptance.

I practice appreciation. That's one way to experience unconditional love today. I appreciate *whatever is* and I appreciate the opportunity to experience *whatever is*, regardless of my feelings about it. I don't need to like something to appreciate it. But I do need to focus to practice appreciation. That's an unchanging vibrational frequency I want to own. It's a life stance I choose because it works for me. (In addition to being greedy, I'm also selfish.) I want the very best life I can live and I'll do my part in creating that life.

For my own benefit I practice appreciation and acceptance. I may not like *what is* but I can always accept it. Acceptance is saying Yes to *what is* and staying present in the moment. Acceptance is practicing humility and being open to learn. Acceptance is trusting life more than we trust our intellect. Acceptance of *what is* releases our wish to push against life. **We trust a wisdom greater than our mind's**.

Surrender describes this attitude. At my core I am Source Energy but I have lots to learn. Fortunately, I have the best teacher in this or any world. Life wants me to learn and is always offering me opportunities — little ones and larger ones — but I'm only given the precise next step for which I'm ready.

I admit that I am a slow learner. When an old belief directs my thinking, I don't notice alternative ways of thinking. I learned very young not to expect or to count on love. I learned that when love presented itself, it soon vanished. So I learned not to trust love. Better to withdraw than to be pushed away, a decision that makes sense only to a vulnerable child but one that formed the wallpaper of my adult experience.

Accepting Unconditional Love

Against this background of disappointment and loneliness, I impose my choice to receive Source's absolute and unwavering unconditional love. A lovely theory. Sounds grand.

But what does it mean? And how do I open to receive love after having practiced (unknowingly) avoiding love for decades?

I diminished my childhood vulnerability by closing off my wants but now I need to embrace vulnerability to allow Source to operate powerfully in my life and in my body. **I can't avoid any part of me and receive Source**. I can't hide and I can't pretend. I need to appreciate every tiny detail about myself. I need to appreciate me.

Source adores me. Easy for Source. Source adores everyone. A fact which doesn't tarnish my particular experience of Source. I'm not another one of billions of annoying children running in circles. I am unique and, in that way, special.

I experience myself as an expression of Source, mightily.

It's not because I am good enough but because I allow. Source is always present and waiting for an opening. The MS diagnosis tore a huge opening in me. Now I'm grateful for that.

Although it was an unwelcome condition, I don't focus on the condition but on the vibrational frequency of perfect health. That diagnosis doesn't prevent me from experiencing perfect health. In fact, it motivates me to choose health consciously.

I take responsibility for my current state of health, not in a self-deprecatory way, but as a snap shot of how I have lived. There has been too much hurt. Of course, my body will reflect that stress. Could I have handled it differently? I don't see how. I did the best I knew at each juncture.

I don't criticize myself for being where I am now health-wise. This is a wonderful opportunity to watch Source heal me in a way I can't heal myself. I haven't a clue about how healing will happen in my body but I don't doubt that healing is happening now and will continue to happen. At some point it will manifest. I'm already walking better and standing straighter.

In my inner world, I choose alignment with Source over and over throughout the day. That's putting in an order for magic and committing to allow that magic to work in my life. I don't understand magic but I'm open to it. It's my best hope.

And not such a puny hope, either. We fall back on Source when we can't effect the change we want by ourselves. As with any independent three year old we say, "I'll do it myself." It doesn't take long before we're out of good ideas and hope and confidence in our own ability. How perfect surrender is at that point!

And, really, we don't want to surrender before then. Inviting Source to heal us has to be our very last resort or we haven't reached the depth of vulnerability that's required to allow healing.

But once we embrace that vulnerability and then do it again and again and again, we realize it's a great place to live. We're more alive when we're anchored in our vulnerability. We live closer to our core. We're clear about what is really important. And we choose process over fact.

Healing is the process of accepting Source's unconditional love for us each day. We practice receiving when we make decisions about how we spend our time, what we put into our bodies, how we speak, and how we think. I say I choose to experience my oneness with Source and I want to experience complete healing so I won't contaminate my vibrational practice with resentment. I always want to stay in the present moment where I am available to receive. Nothing exists except this moment. I want to make the most of my experience right here, right now by paying attention and by practicing presence.

Source meets me and accepts me and heals me in this moment. I want to show up. I trust, I'm present, and, joyfully, I climb on the Source train which goes I-don't-know-where and on which I will experience I-don't-know-what, and I say Yes enthusiastically and wholeheartedly.

Passion is the only response to Source. Nothing held back, nothing restrained. I am completely here this second — fears, distortions, and all. I present myself and I accept that Source always says **Yes** to me. I have Source's attention this second. And Source sees me whole and healthy. Source accepts me as I am this second, practicing the vibration I choose this second. The past doesn't exist. Only this second counts. Then life shows me my next step. All I need do is pay attention and allow.

Chapter Eleven

Why is it so hard for us to trust that the Universe is benevolent and pulling us to our best? If we did trust, we would live joyfully. Every day would be a party as we anticipate receiving more gifts.

Many of us live as though life is a chore. We work at jobs we don't love just to pay the bills. We count the days to retirement as though we're being released from prison. But we carry our prisons with us. We don't say what we think out of fear of the reaction we'll receive. We don't risk thinking for ourselves. We don't even want to know what we feel unless it's benign. It seems that we don't want to be too well-defined.

Would we operate that way if we trusted that we are loved and valued and unique and needed?

We act like we hate our uniqueness; we blame our constriction on society, the group, the church, tradition, anything but our fear. For if we truly accepted Source's unconditional love for us, how could we do anything but celebrate? If we felt Source's constant encouragement, would we hold ourselves back?

And why don't we feel Source's consistent love and support and encouragement and joy for us?

We choose to block it. What a responsibility it would be for any one of us to carry if we truly believed that who we are counts. If we are just one more undeserving loser, we relieve ourselves of the burden to care about ourselves. And if we don't care about ourselves, how can we imagine that Source cares for us?

Choosing self-hate (to a lesser or greater degree) we rationalize as noble. We believe that that motivates us to grow but in truth it prevents growth. Growth is allowing Source to work in us with all the magic and mystery that implies. But self-hate shuts us down. We are resigned to live in a diminished, less than exuberant manner. We don't want too much. We feel mature about being realistic with our very limited expectations. And we're not sorely disappointed any more.

We tolerate health that is less than optimal. We accept a constricted life. We're satisfied to act like others and we want to think that really we <u>are</u> like others. We don't want to know ourselves in much depth. We relate to ourselves at arm's length, as though we stand outside ourselves and look at ourselves instead of anchoring deeply inside. We become objects to ourselves and we critique ourselves as object, assessing our value, comparing our contributions. We reduce our aliveness. And, thereby, we hope we will be better persons!?!?

Why the determination to live a small life?

The challenges of surviving overwhelm a powerless child. Understandably, s/he seeks safety. But why as adults do we still cling to safety instead of choosing to experience all that life offers? Why do we still think of ourselves as powerless?

We cannot supply power for ourselves, we can only recognize it. Power lives in our deepest Source Energy center. We don't create it; we only allow it. There are certain rules that allow us to experience Source Energy power which is Source's unconditional love for us.

The first is that we recognize how we block ourselves from receiving Source's love for us. We don't have to do anything differently, we just have to see the truth of *what is*. That, in itself, sends most folks scurrying. When we sit in meditation and we notice our thoughts and our feelings from our Observer standpoint, we invite healing. We don't have to accept guilt for *what is* inside us right now, we just notice. We show up and we allow the Universe to work in us and we observe. That's all.

In the Observer we don't have an agenda. We notice *what is* with our thoughts and our feelings. We don't identify with our thoughts or our feelings or another's judgment of us. We stay present to our process in the moment and we allow.

These sound like simple instructions: show up, stay out of the way, and allow. How do we get it so wrong?

When we're born we know what we feel and what we want and we accept ourselves. We broadcast our wishes loudly and immediately. We don't learn to distance ourselves from our feelings until we experience ourselves in relationship with someone more powerful than we are and upon whom we depend. Gaining that person's favor is crucial since they control our world. If they are unresponsive, we lose. If they withdraw, even temporarily, we lose. If they react angrily, we lose. We need them to stay calm and to pay attention to us so that we can receive what we need to survive.

Before we know what is what, we can discern our caregiver's preferences. The parts of us s/he doesn't like we learn to dislike. Whatever it is about us that threatens receiving love, we will diminish. "If Mom doesn't like some part of me, there clearly is something wrong with me because she's powerful and I am not." We defer to the powerful other and we abandon ourselves. We don't know we're doing this initially but we continue to diminish ourselves throughout our young lives. Whatever damage we do to ourselves is worth it if we can be seen as more loveable by the powerful authority. We increase our value by diminishing our uniqueness.

And that's how we learn to treat ourselves as object. We look at ourselves through another's eyes. We evaluate who we are and we judge ourselves as (we think) others judge us. We move away from our vulnerable core. We're not as easily hurt. We cut off our sensitivity. We learn how to stay in control, especially if vulnerability has been traumatic for us.

And the more we're in control, the less we feel Source in our lives. We experience Source through our feelings. If we resist our feelings, we lose connection with Source. If we allow our feelings to carry us wherever we need to go inside us, we open to Source. We can't be "altogether" and "in control" and simultaneously available to Source.

As adults when we open to feel our feelings and to allow them to be, we invite an experience of congruence in the present moment. We may stay behind the Observer window. We may choose to practice detachment. But we notice our feelings and we experience our feelings at the same time. We may fear the intensity of our feelings but from behind the Observer window, we notice that, too.

We appreciate any art which pulls us to feel deeply. We long to reunite with the scary parts of ourselves but we can't always do so directly. We know something is missing. We cut off our feelings but then we can't find our souls. We pursue dramatic outer world adventures in our search for what will complete us. We use drugs. We work excessively. We overdo anything in hopes that something outside us will restore our wholeness.

It's Source we seek and it's Source we fear.

We think about Source and we read and we practice rituals and we listen to authorities. But still something eludes us. We desperately long for Source's unconditional acceptance and love. We try to understand intellectually what we long to experience emotionally. We fear opening our hearts. We don't accept ourselves and we don't want to experience wholly what it is to be ourselves. We create a straightjacket life for ourselves. With our lack of self-acceptance, our longing for Source's unconditional love, and our fear of feeling our feelings, we can't move.

Once in a while we may notice that we seem to be living a perfect day. We love it and acknowledge that we wish every day were like this. But we sabotage ourselves repeatedly . And we don't know that we're the ones keeping ourselves apart from receiving Source's unconditional love. We think we do our best. We're nice and we can be generous and we are always appropriate. But we ache inside. What we need, we resist. And it kills our souls.

Chapter Twelve

We resist Source's love by trying to figure out how we keep ourselves apart from Source. We use our intellect to try to bridge a gap that was created by using our intellect. Our intellect grounded in our human center can only solve problems. Our perceived separation from Source is not a problem to be solved but a condition to be healed.

In truth there is no separation, not from Source's side. But our intellects have been so busy and so active in devising strategies to keep us safe and enhance our worth, that we lose touch with our Essence. In our eternal Essence we are one with Source. Our Essence exists right now. We didn't create it and we can't destroy it. It is our foundation.

We can move into our Essence any moment we choose and experience our oneness with Source immediately. That's always available to us. We can't think our way into our Essence but we allow ourselves to be carried there when we practice stillness. Inevitably, we move into our core when we leave our intellect at the door and practice surrender.

So, why doesn't everyone do this all the time? Or at least some of the time?

Source is here and is available and knows exactly what we need and can provide that for us this second. It's free and doesn't require muscle or smarts or cheeriness. Do we get a better offer ever?

And yet we hesitate. We'd rather think. Which is the opposite of what we need to do.

We need to practice resonance between ourselves in our human center and ourselves in our eternal center. We make peace with where we are this second and we allow ourselves to be just as we are. We may notice frustration on the other side of the Observer window but we stay on the Observer side, detached and alert and present. And we breathe and we focus on this second.

And then we do it again.

That's the recipe for opening to Source. Daily practice helps immensely.

We move into our eternal center and we see as Source sees, with no criticism, no expectation, no judgment. We practice staying behind the Observer window. We notice and we allow. We practice surrender and we trust.

And then we watch.

Life will bring our lessons to us. We pay attention, we notice our resistance, and we give ourselves time to be still.

In our stillness we notice Source moving in our lives. We notice coincidences and unplanned but perfect meetings that could only happen in the minute. We notice how what we want but don't express verbally comes to us. We notice that our thoughts in one minute anticipate the words we hear in the next. We notice and we allow. We appreciate and we marvel. And that's all.

We learn the rhythm of surrender and we allow life to carry us.

Chapter Thirteen

After meditating this afternoon I know more surely than ever that my perfect walking comes to me. I'm not seeing it manifest at this moment, but the experience of hanging out in my eternal center during meditation reassures me that what I want already exists vibration ally. The crucial variable in this process seems to be spending time in my eternal center, allowing. Otherwise, I have only my thoughts and my feelings.

Fear has haunted me all my life; today I see it clearly from behind the Observe window. I'm glad that I can discern the fear while practicing detachment. All I need do is stay behind my Observer window in meditation and it will be healed. I'm always amazed by the depth of the inner world. So much of what we're unaware forcefully influences our experience. So, when I see my fear, I'm grateful. I know I'm moving to a deeper level inside myself and allowing healing at greater depth.

My healing is happening. I trust it and I watch. I know for sure that it will continue. I'm doing my own inner work which is the consciousness basis for health. I notice the fear, I experience it without identifying with it. I allow it to be healed through practicing vibrational alignment with my Source Energy center which knows perfect health for me. I know this process is healing me on physical and emotional levels.

At some point in the future I will be so happy and proud and grateful and humble when my healing manifests. I'll practice that vibration now.

Chapter Fourteen

In my second meditation yesterday I saw how deeply some of my beliefs and fears lie. So deep that they didn't originate as mine. And then I saw huge garden shears clipping them all, the ribbons tying me to the past floating away. I felt so free. I felt transcendent. I could rise above those old constrictions and truly feel joy.

The pope's visit this week has been televised. He seems like such an open-hearted, loving person. Today I know what that feels like. He was the image that fit my experience of being transcendent, that flowing non-reactive clarity.

Meditation makes this all so clear quickly and easily. But only at the right moment. I practice the truth of my perfect healing and perfect walking. Then each step to my desire shows itself to me in its own time.

I also saw how my fear of the world is illusory. I fantasize horrors as a child might but the truth is I can keep myself safe from abuse by other humans. I can see what's happening and change the situation with my words or by removing myself. I'm not helpless or dependent. My Adult vowed to my Scared Child that she will always protect her. Today my Adult is strong enough.

At lunch my friend Laurie reminded me that healing can happen instantaneously. I stood up and walked well though not far. I appreciate her confirming faith.

My body has carried tension, maybe from birth. I release that tension when I feel my feelings. As a child I tried to change a Controller into an Appreciator of me. How controlling is that?! As an adult I need to be what I want — self-accepting, happy, open, and appreciating myself.

For two days I have been mired in some heaviness I couldn't identify. Now I see that my challenge is to accept the Controller instead of making it wrong. I've written so much about the Controller for many years; the war inside me between my Controller and my Child threatened to do me in. As I clarify the dynamics inside me which are enacted around me, I see them and release them. I feel lighter and healthier.

In yesterday's meditation I felt led to walk at Home Depot. I haven't walked there for months. I walked well for ten minutes and stopped when I felt my legs tiring. Today I walked for fifteen minutes and again stopped when my legs started to tire. This is so exciting! It's no coincidence that my stronger walking follows my acceptance of my Controller whom I have demonized.

Then I saw the neurologist. He is satisfied with my progress and gives all the credit to the meds. That's OK. He insisted that there is still a lot I can do in the gym (a reflection of my Controller driving me). I know that isn't true nor is it how my healing guides me.

I feel shakier and less clear after having spoken with the neurologist than I have for months. He says I'll be taking the meds forever. I feel less hopeful about my complete healing and less like myself and less anchored in what I know is my truth. I feel like a rug has been pulled out from under me. His vibes seeped inside me. I'll have to work to restore my own balance. My afternoon client canceled as did my client tomorrow morning. I'm faced with lots of free time and some inner work to do. The Universe supports me in doing my work.

Spending time alone and in quiet benefits me. I need the neurologist for medication but I won't lose my own vision for my future. I appreciate what he can do for me but that really is a very small part of my healing,

I forgive my Controller (and other Controllers). I appreciate them for being just where they are. I accept that they will never know me and that they don't even want to. And that's truly OK. I win if I love them. As a child I had wanted them to love me. The ball's in my court, though. I don't need to wrest anything from another person. I just need to appreciate them no matter where they are. When I do that, I feel great and I win.

Chapter Fifteen

I'm so grateful that meditation has taught me detachment from my feelings. When old intense feelings arise as a result of practicing presence, I know that I am healing. I know that all I need do is allow. I know that the Universe is working in my life in ways I don't understand but in ways I totally trust. I welcome healing. I don't understand it or feel comfortable with it but I know my inner world. I know it works in ways my mind can't describe. I know it heals what I don't even know needs to be healed. And I trust the Universe to heal me.

Lately, I've noticed old familiar feelings. I don't know when they arose originally but the words today that describe these feelings are that I don't have a place in the world. I feel small, powerless, overwhelmed, and vulnerable. I haven't felt these feelings for decades but when they surfaced near bed time and during the night, I recognized their pull. When I was young these feelings plagued me. This time I watched them, I felt their power but I wasn't unsettled. I practiced detachment. I know there is nothing I need to do. It's not a problem that requires action. It's the Universe guiding me to my healing.

The Universe knows better than I do where I am, where I want to be, and how I need to get there. It's not a path I can imagine. I didn't know that these feelings still live deeply inside me. It doesn't matter what I know or don't know. **All that matters is that I maintain a stance of allowing and trust**.

I so very much want my brain MRI to reveal fewer or no brain lesions. I've been told that's impossible medically. So, if that's what I want, I must trust the Universe to show me how to get there. I know that the Universe is unlimited in what it can do and, when it operates through me, I participate in the unlimitedness. I'm very clear about the healing I want. I know the Universe understands me and wants to support me. My part is to cooperate by allowing the Universe to do its work in me. That's one definition of accepting Source's love for me.

I admit that my feelings can be intense and painful and scary. I suspect that some folks would resist them. Certainly, while I move through these feelings I feel separated from others. Yesterday I couldn't make adequate contact with anyone I spoke to. I felt misunderstood. I felt offended by some reactions I received but I took it as simply my experience of being unable to connect.

This morning in my meditation I realized that I am being led down my own specifically individual path. No one else travels this path with me. That's OK. I know myself well enough to trust my journey but I can't explain my experience to others or even share it. No one else has experienced these feelings in the way that I am right now. I know that my inner world is the basis for everything that happens to me. I want a lot so I'll go through whatever it takes to allow healing in my inner world.

I want complete healing of the MS. (I don't label it my MS; I'm not holding on to it.) I suspect that someone has already allowed healing of a diagnosis considered un-healable. But I will allow myself to be guided to healing in my own terms.

This week my walking has improved significantly. I'm cautious and not pushing myself. I accept no impulses from my Controller. I pray before I go out. I felt guided in meditation to return to Home Depot. I walked slowly and precisely and I stopped when my legs started to tire. Four times this week I walked a little and a little farther and then farther still. The biggest change I notice is that my legs seem to be growing stronger. My endurance increases. That hasn't happened in years. For the last ten months I've noticeably

Accepting Unconditional Love

weakened after exercising but now I'm not pushing. When I do walk, my muscles feel stronger the next day. A huge change. And the release of another limitation.

I feel unlimited at times. I feel Source's light at my center and I'm thrilled by the opportunity to heal completely. It's without any mental input from my Controller or any direction from outside me. I'm so glad to do something unique and to allow healing my way.

The solitariness is OK. How much depth can I experience with others present? It seems that my achievements and my contributions come from my willingness to spend time with my inner world. I feel more at home there. My inner world makes more sense to me than the outer world. When the outer world proves frustrating I look to my inner world to help me understand what's happening.

I'm so glad my meditations prove to be illuminating and that they guide me so precisely. It took commitment to learn to meditate well but it has opened the world to me. I'm very grateful that this clarity is available to us humans.

I practice accepting Source's love for me by allowing Source to work in me to heal.

The truth is my perfect health. Any fear is unnecessary.

Chapter Sixteen

I'm so fortunate to face this challenge and to partner with Source to open doors to my healing. I'm so glad I have been tagged with a label I didn't want. I love employing Source magic to heal what looks impossible to heal.

Chapter Seventeen

When I chose to major in Psychology in college I wanted to understand life. Now after more than 40 years of clinical work I realize that I don't really seek understanding. I want depth and passion and immersion. Experience is the key. Experience is not what happens to us but our perceptions of ourselves and our processing of what happens. Experience is allowing ourselves to be touched.

Nothing is determined. Is one event bad or good? It's neither. Is one circumstance better than another? What is, just is. We can learn about ourselves by moving through our experience or we can reinforce our resistance to life. It's about **practicing availability**.

Our foundational question: Do we trust life or do we resist it? It seems a simple question but it isn't. We need to recognize and accept Universal laws. We learn those laws by paying attention to our experience. That sounds easy enough but I notice that many folks don't open to learn. It's as though they already know How-Life-Is, what they can expect, and what their place is. I've noticed that <u>we</u> determine how life is, what we can expect, and what our place is by our openness or by our defensiveness.

We are available when we allow ourselves to feel; we're not available when we think. We are available when we open to learn; we're not available when we already know the answers. We're not available when we cease questioning and wondering. We are available when we don't know our limits.

So, knowing Source is not a religious concern but a way of approaching our life experience. How can we know reality if we cling to our sense impressions? Our five senses tell us very little about reality in depth and nothing about reality in personal terms. I've learned that experience is totally personal and precisely the best teacher for each of us. My truth is not your truth. We each anchor in our own experience.

We structure our openness to life by how much we trust our feelings to lead us. If, unconsciously, we've closed off our feelings we've lost an important guidance system. Some folks when they are young suffer trauma at the hands of another more powerful figure. They can't handle their desperation and their fear so they shut their feelings down. It's an understandable decision for a child. When we're older we need to heal that early trauma and restore our wholeness which we have damaged by our choice to avoid our feelings.

We heal our traumas and our wounds by feeling our feelings. We can't handle the intensity when we are young but we need to handle it when we are older. We don't want to live our adult lives by decisions we made in our powerless childhood. But that is how many of us travel through life. We don't depend on childhood decisions anywhere else in our daily activities — we're open to learning new technologies, to earning advanced degrees, and to excelling in our fields of endeavor. But our inner worlds remain the mystery to us that they were in childhood. And we lose so much by clinging to that immaturity and fear.

Our feelings usher us into our inner worlds. Our inner worlds hide in shadows until we learn to recognize the subtle directional markers. Eventually, we can discern the imbalance in our inner world relationships (Critic/Child or Artist/Controller or Hard Worker/Playmate or Abuser/Victim) even though imbalance feels right initially. We learn that seeking comfort instead of meeting challenges keeps us immature. We acknowledge that our critical relatives reflect our own inner world Critic to us. We learn the self-discipline of using good judgment when we choose to identify with the Moderate Adult instead of the Self-indulgent Child.

Our psychological subpersonalities heal and grow when we provide them with the nurturance they have lacked. **Growing**

psychologically leads us into growth spiritually. The two realms of reality, the psychological and the spiritual, are not separate. It is neither noble nor mature to "tough it out" in response to uncomfortable feelings. Our feelings grab our attention. Then we move into our inner worlds and notice the action there. And, always, there is something going on in our inner worlds.

I'm all for joy and peace and contentment. When that's what your inner world offers you, luxuriate in that experience. But there is no need to fear or to avoid what is uncomfortable or unexpected. Behind sadness is some truth personally meaningful for you. When you stay present to it and allow it to carry you, you will experience healing and growth. Your feelings carry you to a deeper place of wisdom. Always we pay attention to our feelings.

Sometimes it's appropriate to think. To maneuver through the day or to strategize a plan of action, we want to think, especially, if our hearts are uninvolved. We never use our heads to quell uncomfortable feelings by demeaning another person or ourselves. We don't convert feelings into thoughts. We don't pretend with ourselves. We tell ourselves the truth about what we feel and we allow ourselves to pay attention to and experience our feelings.

When we judge a part of ourselves as unworthy or unwanted, we damage our wholeness. When we allow another to do so, we accept abuse, we internalize it, and eventually we abuse ourselves. The way we treat ourselves internally (without anyone's awareness) influences our experience of Source. When we deny our vulnerability or our confusion or our anger, we diminish our integrity, our experience of our wholeness. When we do that, and we usually do it unconsciously, we refuse Source's unconditional acceptance of us.

The fact that some of our decisions are unconscious (made without our awareness) doesn't relieve us of our responsibility for the consequences of those decisions. I wonder about my own responsibility for inviting MS. Certainly, it wasn't conscious. I've exercised and eaten appropriately. I've used good judgment about choosing behaviors that support me. But in my early life I couldn't handle the frustration and sadness and loneliness and hurt of being me. I needed support which I didn't receive so I changed myself in order to (hopefully) hurt less. I thought I would be more acceptable if I were different, specifically, less emotional. This example of childish thinking seems innocent but has severe implications. Too young to believe in myself, I trusted others who didn't believe in me. I learned to hate parts of myself which I was taught were defective. I tried to destroy those parts to make life more comfortable.

Of course, the rewards were minimal and intermittent. Nevertheless, I damaged myself in ways I didn't know or understand. I can accept that I invited MS by my lack of self-acceptance.

This statement is not logical. I've only come to this realization after thousands of hours of meditating. I'm not angry with myself. Rather, I understand completely how that early pain was funneled into my body where I could more easily ignore it.

Indirectly, I closed myself off from Source's love and acceptance. I tried to be acceptable in behavioral and intellectual terms to folks around me; I lost my heart and my wholeness in the process. I thought truth was outside me and someone else would give it to me. I distrusted my own experience.

After studying Psychology, working with my inner world dynamics, meditating, and journal writing, I noticed an integration of my inner world experience. I grew to know myself in depth, to feel the layers of my feelings, and to allow my feelings to heal, to forgive others who didn't support me, and to rely upon my inner world resources. Now I look for guidance in life, which is to say Source. I know how to recognize life beckoning to me and I pay attention. I truly accept that I am loved more than I have ever loved myself. I revel in that truth.

All of this delving and studying and working and paying attention is how I know reality. What is reality and how does reality operate? I started with the personal psychological dynamics and moved through deeper and deeper layers of my inner world until I found Source at my deepest center.

Knowing Source is knowing reality. Cutting off parts of ourselves distorts reality. Accepting Source's unconditional love opens us to know all of reality.

The key is saying Yes. Yes to acknowledging *what is* inside me and outside me. And Yes to me. Now I know that I am valuable and that my inner world is worth paying attention to. I deserve my attention. And I know that I am guided every day. Walking in partnership with Source is a fabulous, fun, exciting, profound way to live. Every day I discover gifts and surprises and confirmations and, always, more guidance. All this joy follows from accepting every part of myself and, thus, allowing Source's acceptance of me.

Chapter Eighteen

A question we each need to answer is: In how much depth do I want to experience Source? Stated another way: How deeply do I want to know myself?

Source is to be experienced. Source isn't a figure modeled after a parent. Source is a presence. Source is. We humans want to imagine Source in our own likeness but we can only know Source through experience. Source isn't an individual — all holy, perfect, complete, and judgmental. Source is an ever-moving flow. We can allow the flow to carry us or we can resist it.

We resist Source when we narrow our experience. If we don't want to experience ourselves with depth, we insist that reality is only what we can see and touch. We may choose to stay in our heads, thinking about Source or life or reality instead of experiencing Source/life/reality. We may want to make life logical and predictable so we disregard the fear behind our want. If we can organize our thinking, we assure ourselves that we are safe.

Choosing safety eliminates the openness necessary to experience Source in depth.

Safety implies a reduction in vitality. If life has been scary or painful when we were powerless, we do what we can to artificially construct a sense of power and to diminish our vulnerability. If we maintain a powerless mindset, we don't naturally grow into our power. We stay stuck in the Controller and we never open to our experience which leads to healing.

When we prefer to think and refuse to feel, we can't experience Source; we can only talk about Source. When we don't want to practice presence to ourselves in depth, we can't practice presence to Source.

Source is the most basic part of us and the least predictable.

If we'd prefer that Source be "other" and outside ourselves, we shelter ourselves from the depths of our experience of our own being and of our own life. It's easier to have an all-powerful parent figure who is different from us. If we acknowledge our Essence as Source, we hesitate. We can't disregard our core if Source lives in us. We can't write off our experience and dismiss our feelings. When we accept Source as our basis, we pay attention to every detail of our experience. When we trust that Source pays attention to us, we can't devalue ourselves.

It's our responsibility, and a most joyful one at that, to know ourselves in depth. It's the opposite of being self-absorbed. Acknowledging our Source core humbles us. We respect our curiosity because it leads us into our deepest unexplored territory where no one else can travel. Knowing Source in depth makes our experience meaningful in completely personal terms. My experience of Source in the second is probably not your experience. After all, my challenges are not yours. Experiencing Source is not objective. We learn the attitudes to practice which allow an experience of Source, but we can't program that experience.

Source guides us to the perfect next step for our own personal growth and healing. The guidance isn't the same for our neighbor and it can't be mapped. We are individuals and Source knows us precisely. We know ourselves by opening to Source. We appreciate the wisdom of our oneness.

We learn to see all of life as one fabric. What we experience or choose to deny isn't our secret. It affects what happens to us and what others say to us. Our responsibility extends far beyond our behavior. We ignore our inner worlds only to invite the outer world to impact us. For we will be shown the truth. We can accept it or we can deny it.

Another level of not opening to Source is by intellectualizing. We may prefer to know ourselves above the neck exclusively and to avoid life's messiness. Some of us practice compartmentalization when we quote an authority and try to fit ourselves into the authority's box. That way we don't live our days with too much intensity. We lean on the padding another's words give us and we mold ourselves from the outside instead of allowing ourselves to be pulled from our center. Source is replaced by rules. When we focus on following the rules we distance ourselves from experiencing Source (and Source's love for us). We make life fit into small boxes and, thereby, we reduce our anxiety.

We humans try to make Source palatable, as though we swallow Source in small sugary bites. We want to be right and to do life right and we want to know Source as someone else describes Source. We want to trust something outside ourselves. And by doing so, we refuse to experience Source.

Our experience of Source is completely personal. It doesn't fit in a box and it isn't formatted in a self-help book. Our experience is uniquely ours. We don't need validation from anyone else. Most likely no one else can understand where we are internally and no one's intellect can offer us the clarity which is specific to us. We love inspiring talks, but experiencing Source is momentary and non-intellectual and founded upon embracing our vulnerability.

We anchor in our Source experience when we make "I" statements. We refer to our truth inside and accept responsibility for our own perceptions and feelings and needs. We don't judge or imitate others. We choose not to make controlling "You" statements or to presume that we know what is best for another. We are humble to our core and we love our humility for that's how we invite Source to guide us on this adventure which is life.

Initially, we focus on our individual experience. We know what we are feeling, we allow our feelings, and we practice detachment. By doing so, we notice our inner world imbalances and dynamics.

Our insights seem totally personal. We appreciate the mystery and the power of our inner worlds. We practice presence which invites the Universe to work in our lives.

We notice what happens to us in the world with other folks and we realize that there is correlation between our inner and outer worlds. At that point we move from the strictly personal experience of Source to the awareness of Source working in the world around us. By allowing healing inside us, we invite healing in a communal realm. We experience Source in the world, drawing encounters to us. These encounters frequently unsettle us. It's easy to point to their unfairness. But we trust that these experiences carry us to a new level of healing and, gladly, we cooperate with life. We recognize ourselves as partners with Source. We pay attention to our daily experiences. We recognize co-creation and we enjoy playing with Source.

We notice the seamless fabric of life. What happens to us reflects our inner world dynamics. We lose our resentment and reject victim thinking. Even with the most horrible occurrences we say, "I made this happen with my consciousness. I'll take responsibility and notice how I did that."

When we accept this level of reality, we've moved into a transpersonal realm. We don't struggle or blame or deny. Nor do we hate ourselves. Whatever happens to us shows us our creative power.

We all have a Victim subpersonality who doesn't own her power. That's fine. We can stay in our Observer and notice this figure. As long as we notice the internal dynamics, we don't act them out unconsciously.

I learned a huge lesson about the seamlessness of my experience 40 years ago. At 26 I had received my doctorate in Psychology. An additional 1500 hours of post-graduate clinical work qualified me to sit for the state licensing exam. At 27 I passed the written section and faced the orals.

My Controller had always pushed me to achieve and to achieve early. I had started school at four, graduated from college at 20, spent nine months recovering from a viral infection in my spinal fluid, received my Master's degree at 22, worked for a year in a psychiatric hospital, and earned my doctorate at 26. It felt like a relentless whirlwind. I forged ahead at every step.

I faced my ultimate professional dream at 27 — to take the written and oral exams to receive a state license to practice as a Clinical Psychologist. I couldn't imagine anything better. I had worked all my life to be at this point.

I passed the written exam but I didn't recognize my reluctance to take the next step, sitting for the orals. My Controller had tolerated no hesitation at any point in my academic career. In my 20's I didn't identify my Controller or realize that this wasn't the way everyone lived. I knew I was driven but that wasn't a problem. The fact that sleep eluded me and that I preferred work to play seemed acceptable. I could live with the imbalance and, in fact, I wanted to. My Controller wanted to, anyway. Another part of me resisted. But I identified with my Controller and ignored other parts.

I failed the orals. I was devastated. My Controller was furiously angry with me. I didn't value any other part of me at that time so I didn't recognize it as an internal conflict. I felt ashamed and disappointed with myself. There was no gentleness or compassion inside me, only abuse.

After a week when I had suffered miserably, I went to bed in my second floor apartment. At midnight I awoke, terrified to realize that someone had broken in. My first thought was of the dream I had dreamt for years about exactly this scenario. "So this was what that dream was about, " I thought. The intruder entered my bedroom, surprised I was there, and attacked me.

Mentally, I was destroyed by that experience for months. I lost my sense of self and of having boundaries. I couldn't focus my attention and I definitely couldn't achieve. Survival became the daily goal, not progress.

No one would say that I consciously invited this horrible experience. I was in my apartment with the door locked, asleep in the dark. Behaviorally, I could not be held culpable. Clearly, I was a victim.

After meditating and recognizing my inner world dynamics, I identified my responsibility in drawing this event to me. My Controller's ire was acted out. I couldn't simply accept a victim role and feel sorry for myself. My Controller's punishment was brutal, but that is what living with my Controller was like at the time.

It took me years to work through the trauma. Then I had to forgive myself for unconsciously orchestrating the event. If I practice that intense anger and hatred for myself, the Universe finds a similar vibration and draws it to me. My outer world experience showed me my inner world experience. And inside is always where experience starts.

I know what it is to be a victim. I don't blame victims for their situations. But I know that unconscious dynamics play out interpersonally. I felt empowered by recognizing my part in creating the situation. I never underestimate the power of my inner world. And I appreciate the consistency of my inner and outer world experience.

It's a blessing to see so clearly. Clarity is the goal of our work in knowing Source. Source is everything. What I experience of Source is what I pull to me. I can take responsibility for that or not. But knowing reality clearly is being open to know Source. Source isn't a kindly grandfather who indulges us. Source is the vibrational fabric of our minute-by-minute experience. Whatever vibration we practice, Source will reflect to us. We can't choose denial and then say we're open to knowing Source. But we can experience the beauty and consistency and magic in creating with Source. Regardless of what we create, there's nothing better than knowing we're creating in partnership with Source. And nothing more confirming.

Chapter Nineteen

Our job is to appreciate.

Not to explain why natural disasters happen or to philosophize about the nature of being or even to understand what we feel. We simply show up, we notice *what is*, we realize that we are receiving a gift in experiencing *whatever is* this second, and we say, Thank You. No matter how it feels, this second can pull us to healing. We embrace that healing if we pay attention and if we practice humility.

That's not easy, especially when others have been discourteous or inappropriate. But the point of our life experience is not to be right or to demand fairness. We are here to learn and to grow. We grow when we adopt a detached stance and we notice. Choosing to practice vibrational alignment leads us to experience upheaval and surprise. We go along for the ride; we don't criticize the ride. When we commit to partnership with Source, we buy the ticket. We just don't know where the ride takes us. But that's really OK because we trust Source more than we trust our intellect. We don't mind temporary discomfort in the service of our healing and wholeness.

This game of life is so much larger and more intricate than any one of us can imagine. We are honored to participate. With our limited imaginations we can't possibly envision what is best for us and definitely we can't see how to get there. All we can know is the next step and we know that only by practicing humility and paying attention and appreciating *what is* this second.

Maggie had an outpatient surgical procedure this week. Everything non-surgical went wrong. She didn't receive the attention or the support she wanted from the medical staff both before and after the surgery. She felt hurt by the lack of respect she was shown. She knew their behavior was unprofessional and she was understandably angry.

But Maggie meditates. She knows that scrims of distortion cover her perceptions, as is true for all of us. She identified with her Observer. Though it would have been understandable for her to criticize the participants in her ordeal she chose to focus on her inner world. The immediate intensity of her anger scared her. So, she stayed behind her Observer window and noticed it. Practicing detachment in the face of overwhelming emotion is a skill that takes time and self-discipline to master. Her meditation background served her well.

Even though we say that we practice detaching from our thoughts in meditation, we tend to identify with them when we are stressed. I've found that in ordinary times most new meditators can't notice their thoughts because they still think their thoughts. When we experience unusually powerful feelings, looking at our thoughts challenges anyone.

But thinking, instead of feeling, distorts our inner world healing process. Like pouring our feelings into an insulated cup, thinking prevents us from experiencing the heat. Thus, we don't allow the natural healing flow that follows from feeling our feelings.

When we choose to sit in meditation we say to the Universe, "I am available." We don't resist our own process. We don't avoid our feelings. When we sit every day we invite the Universe to work in us in greater depth. And the Universe always says **Yes**.

And then we gasp. Healing doesn't feel like we had expected. Our life is upended. Clearly, our intellect no longer controls the action. We realize that we've stepped into another realm and we don't know the dimensions or the rules in this arena. We panic.

And this is the point when we trust Source's unconditional love for us. Or not.

Our meditations have carried us deeper inside than we had expected and we can't pretend to operate superficially any more.

Accepting Unconditional Love

Initially, it feels like drowning and it terrifies us. We have lost our lives the way we have known them. We can only tolerate the chaos in our journey because we're open to Source and we trust.

This key point in our journey tests our resolve. We realize that comfort is not possible in the way we've always known comfort — with a measure of denial and avoidance. Now we've jumped in and we can't save ourselves. We trust what we can't see and what we don't understand.

This total trust allows us to receive Source's unconditional love for us. If we hold back and try to act reasonably, we close ourselves off from Source by choosing mundane suffering instead of living with vibrancy. We often wish we had more — vitality, money, love, joy. But when it comes to opening to receive more, we choke. In order to receive at a greater level we must integrate our vulnerability at a greater level. Pretty scary. Unless you meditate and allow and trust.

Meditation shows us the path but not what we will encounter on the path. We move down the path with a focus on this second, practicing acceptance. New meditators expect that walking the path will be easy and turbulence-free. Experienced meditators know that walking the path offers an intensity and a depth and meaning unlike anything else. With no chance of staying in control, we still show up every day and we allow. We hold our ticket in hand and we're committed to take the ride because we choose to experience Source's unconditional love.

From that point we lose our lives as we have known them. As the scrims that distort our clarity are pulled back, we see consistency and meaning in the details of our days. We notice that life responds to our unvoiced thoughts. Sometimes nature plays with us since we have released resistance to just being present.

Some points on the ride feel exhilarating; some don't. If we know we are experiencing Source's unconditional love, we accept and appreciate the opportunities for healing. We don't need to direct the ride because magic carries us. Being scared is normal. We stay behind the Observer window and notice the fear. Always we stay behind the Observer window; whatever we notice and experience moves and changes. That's Source working.

Do you choose to allow Source to work in your life? That's a question you answer every day and every second.

Chapter Twenty

Reality is. We can know reality in its simplest sensate terms — what we can see and touch and hear. Our intellect interprets our experience in this realm. Or we can trust our intuition and open to what we can't see or touch. Or we can allow. We watch the Universe respond to our vibrational practice by drawing opportunities to us to experience that same vibratory frequency around us. We know inner and outer reality in the same depth. If we don't move too far inside, we'll be satisfied with knowing outer reality superficially.

Magic happens when we train our vibrational practice towards clarity in knowing reality in depth. We want to know *what is* and we're willing to be Observers and notice patterns in our experience. We don't impose limits on our perceptions or categorize our experience. We simply pay attention and we allow. This stance implies releasing our Controller orientation.

You are in your Controller when:

you think
you already know the answer
you are sure you are right
you justify your position
you make a "You" statement to another person
you don't want surprises
you judge
you quote an authority

you stay busy
you organize your environment
you value and rely upon what has always been true for others

You are in your Controller when you say:

That's not what I learned.
That doesn't fit my expectations.
I don't want to feel these feelings.
This isn't what I bargained for.
If you change your behavior, I will be happier.
Let's stick with the facts.
That's not fair.
You shouldn't treat me that way.
You make me crazy.
Will you grow up?
Don't be so emotional.
You've ruined my life.
My parents ruined my life.
Why don't they stop that dog from barking?
I don't have to take this.
This is what you should do.
I'll help you.
I hope you didn't go out of your way for me.

Clearly, identifying with our Controller is appropriate some of the time. However, when we want to experience Source's unconditional love, we focus upon a vibrational practice that will allow us to open. Identifying with the Controller does not facilitate experiencing or opening.

Being available to experience requires a vibrational practice which is open-ended. We create a space by paying attention to *what is* in the moment and not to thinking our thoughts. An acceptance of our vulnerability and a trust for Universal healing carry us into a realm our intellects can't enter. That's exciting when you are anchored in Essence in your eternal center and terrifying when you aren't.

Consciously moving into Essence means distancing yourself from any self-identifiers. In Essence you be. You don't know anything and you're open to any development. In advance you agree to accept whatever happens. You commit to stay in Essence regardless of what you notice or experience. You anchor in ever-flowing, ever-changing being and you trust completely.

And you allow.

Experiencing Source's unconditional love depends upon our allowing. That love is always available to us. It doesn't change. Our availability to receive, however, changes.

You may want to notice when you (unconsciously) limit your availability to receive:

when you worry

when you try to control what's appropriately out of your control

when you speak off the top of your head instead of practicing presence

when you live more in the past or the future instead of in this minute

when you identify with your feelings instead of noticing what's behind them

when you take yourself seriously

when you think that your thoughts count

when you compare yourself to anyone else

when you try to insure a particular outcome through the force of your will

when you don't play enough

when you criticize yourself

when you expect the worst

when you practice resentment and not gratitude

when you eat when you're not hungry

when you look to chemicals to change your vibrational practice

when you don't trust the stream of well-being flowing to you

Practicing complete self-acceptance trains us to experience Source's unconditional love. Imagining the possibility of an unrealistic good coming to us moves us into an unlimited vibration. Expecting gifts and miracles indicates that we live in the flow of the stream of well-being. Experiencing joy without reason invites the conditions around us to match our vibrational practice.

Chapter Twenty One

Life happens in seconds. While Source's unconditional love for us maintains, we experience it in seconds. Source doesn't change; our availability to receive Source shifts again and again throughout the day.

Being available to experience Source's unconditional love is all we need to practice and we practice that one second at a time. In meditation we notice our availability by consciously focusing on each second. We shine a light on our vibrational practice and, thereby, increase our awareness of our vibrational frequency. That's good practice for every other second of the day, also. We can check inside and notice our availability whenever we think of it. And then we can choose to practice greater availability or not.

Recognizing which vibration we practice at any particular moment provides the first step in self-awareness. To identify the particular vibration in question, we practice stillness. We move behind the Observer window, we practice detachment, and we notice *what is*. Perhaps we notice our Controller thinking thoughts. We may recognize the feeling that accompanies our identification with our Controller. Maybe we're anxious. Maybe we can't easily maintain focus on this second. Maybe we feel an urgency to change a condition. Identify the vibration that goes with your momentarily prominent subpersonality.

Many of us give our Controller too much time. The Controller tells us to think, not to feel, to stay busy, and always to avoid vulnerability. Notice how you feel when you are identified with your Controller.

Perhaps the subpersonality you unconsciously identify with is your Powerless Child. Your feelings impact your thoughts. You know that you can't have what you want. You know you won't be respected. You feel frustrated. Acting passive-aggressively seems justified.

Maybe your unconscious identification lies with your Hard Worker. You only notice the job to be done. You don't acknowledge your feelings or your wants. Your attention jumps to the future when the task will be complete.

Which subpersonality do you favor? Make up your own label which describes the vibration you commonly practice without the awareness that you do so. This is your default vibration. Without awareness you will gravitate to this vibrational practice.

Your default vibration limits your openness to experience Source's unconditional love for you.

The point of your default vibration is to let you move through the day without staying present. The Controller knows what's expected of her and she plays her role. The Hard Worker only considers the necessities of the job. That intense focus determines her attitude. The Powerless Child maintains beliefs (practiced thoughts) about her efficacy, personally and in the world. She harbors fear and resentment. When you identify with your Powerless Child you practice that mixed and self-defeating vibration without knowing that you do.

Observe your default vibration in motion. Stay behind the Observer window and practice detachment. Notice what goes on in your inner world — your thoughts, feelings, and expectations.

Do you have random spontaneous fantasies throughout the day? What is the most frequent theme?
Do you expect to be mistreated by those you do or do not know?
Do you expect to receive gifts?
Is there a subtle expectation that life will improve?
Or that you are close to losing everything?

What do your thoughts and fantasies tell you about your perceived place in the world?

Do you feel safe?

Do you feel loved?

Do you feel like an Adult who has everything she needs to travel through her days satisfactorily?

Do you expect a surprise to be beneficial or diminishing?

Considering these questions will give you an idea of your current inner world status quo. Don't focus on outer world conditions. They just reflect your inner world vibration. Conditions don't make you happy or unhappy. They result from your experience of happiness or unhappiness which results from your vibrational practice.

Identify your assumptions, not the ones you can easily verbalize but the ones that seem reflective of your experience. Take some time answering these questions:

If a stranger walks up to you on the street, what do you imagine will happen?

If you suddenly lose your job, what do you imagine will happen?

An unexpected knock on the door may lead to what?

If you watched a movie of your life, what do you notice about you, the protagonist, in terms of believing in yourself, respecting yourself, and sabotaging yourself? Notice what belief fits your experience as you look back over your lifetime.

Our assumptions about ourselves and the world usually lie so deeply buried inside us that we can't easily verbalize them. They result in encounters in the world that may surprise us. Whom have you encountered memorably? What did this person show you about your inner world?

How do you finish these sentences?

Love this lifetime has been . . .

I'm disappointed when . . .

When I feel disappointed I . . .

About relationships I've learned that . . .
About money I've learned that . . .
About getting ahead I've learned that . . .
I'm different from other folks in that . . .
I expect . . .

Your assumptions form the foundation for your vibrational practice. Your vibrational practice forms the foundation for your experience both internally and in the world.

You create your reality by your beliefs and your expectations. Write about how you do this. Notice your unexpected encounters this month. How did you (unconsciously) draw them to you?

Chapter Twenty Two

Now that you can identify the vibration you find yourself practicing, learn to allow it to shift at will. In your Observer behind the Observer window, notice *what is*. Your Observer doesn't judge or react but simply notices. In meditation we allow healing by staying present. Our Observer is anchored in this second. From that place we watch our vibrational practice. By staying in our Observer we allow our vibration to resolve and to heal on its own.

During the day when you check in for a second or two and notice that you have fallen into practicing a vibration that doesn't serve you, you can choose to practice another vibration. Get familiar with several vibrations — your Playful Child, your Open-Hearted Friend, your Hero, your Resentful Teenager — and any others you notice. But always know what the vibration of Essence in your eternal center feels like.

At your core you are Essence — eternal, loved and appreciated, always experiencing Source. This vibration already exists in you. You can't fake it or manufacture it. But you can cut yourself off from it. Likewise, you can choose to move into it at will.

You allow yourself to move into Essence by your practice of presence in meditation. Throughout the day you can practice appreciation. All the healing, all the bounty, all the joy, all the love that you want already exist in vibrational form in your Essence. There's no need to beg Source to give anything to you. You already have it. If you cut yourself off from experiencing it, what do you expect Source to do? You are the one making all the choices. If you want to know what you choose, look around you at what exists.

Write:

What exists right now in my life fits me perfectly in that . . .

I don't necessarily like *what is* right now in my life but I take responsibility for creating it. I've done that by . . .

I notice my ambivalence about receiving when I don't receive what I say I want. I limit my ability to receive by . . .

Embracing my vulnerability . . .

What I've learned about being vulnerable is . . .

I spend most of my time in my . . . subpersonality. That serves me by . . . but not by . . .

I would do well to let go of . . .

I hold myself back by . . .

In my ideal self I feel . . . I believe . . .

What keeps me from moving into my ideal self this minute is . . .

And then practice presence, focusing on this second and each additional second. Move into your Observer behind the Observer window. Notice and allow. Repeating this practice for several minutes will carry you into your Essence at your deepest center. Familiarize yourself with that vibration. Practice moving into Essence at will.

Chapter Twenty Three

Forgiveness cleanses us. We may have been offended or even seriously hurt by another's behavior or words. Still we choose forgiveness.

Of course, we feel the pain and, perhaps, some anger. Maybe we have revenge fantasies. We take as long as we need to work through our feelings. We stay behind the Observer window and we notice our feelings; we don't identify with them. We need to process our feelings. We can't choose forgiveness prematurely and pretend that we're at peace. The work of practicing vibrational alignment isn't about imitating how we suspect that an aligned person acts. It's about staying present to our core which is always about allowing healing.

Events happen. We can always learn something from our experience. Ideally, we move through our experience with awareness and with depth. We stay present to our feelings as long as we need to but we don't cling to them. Any feeling that we let ourselves acknowledge and feel passes eventually

When we practice the vibration of Powerless Child or Victim or Resentful Adolescent we hold on to the meaning we give our experience. That (unconsciously) influences our vibrational practice. We strengthen a vibration that doesn't serve us. We point to the event and declare its unfairness and indulge our outrage instead of identifying with the flow at our core. The event probably happened so that we could heal our misaligned vibration, not strengthen it.

We are always given the opportunity to notice what vibration we choose and to reconsider. If we want to establish a new vibrational practice, we're aware of our self-sabotaging default vibration. We don't hate it but we choose not to identify with it. We simply step out of that vibration.

We can't always immerse ourselves in the vibration we choose immediately — Hero or Caring Parent or Stalwart Companion. We can release the ties to the vibration we don't choose. We visualize ribbons holding us to a vibration that may have been understandable in the past but practicing that vibration now doesn't serve us. We cut the ribbons and let them float away. We do this exercise repeatedly as we need to.

We keep ourselves from experiencing Source's unconditional love for us by practicing an irrelevant vibration — any vibration that reduces our presence in this second. If an old Victim vibration hounds you, acknowledge it and choose to move into your Observer. The Observer is a non-resistant state and a step on the way to a vibration you'd prefer. You can always choose Observer no matter what vibration tries to dominate. As long as you are behind the Observer window, it doesn't matter what happens on the other side of the window. You practice detachment and you watch. That's all and that's enough.

Practice moving into your Observer several times a day for thirty seconds. Notice how your Observer vibration feels. Now identify with the thought or feeling that you observe and practice that vibration for thirty seconds. Notice how that feels. Now move back into your Observer for thirty seconds.

Practice choosing your vibration throughout the day. In this sense forgiveness means choosing again. I don't need to resent a Perpetrator if I no longer practice a Victim vibration. If I cling to my Victim vibe, of course, I will rope a Perpetrator into my drama. That just shows me how powerful I am.

When I choose to live from my Hero, no one can diminish my experience regardless of what vibration they practice. In the morning I choose my vibration. I stick with it throughout the day no matter how anyone else acts. When I discover that I've slipped into an unwanted vibration, I choose Observer and then Hero again. The vibration I practice is determined by my choice. No one can deter me from choosing my highest and my best vibration repeatedly.

Chapter Twenty Four

I've noticed that the quality of my walking varies with the vibrational frequency I practice. How I experience the world and myself varies with my subpersonality identification in the moment. The quality of my health reflects my consciousness — my beliefs, my thoughts, and my feelings.

Consciousness is a big word. Feeling is a much smaller word. Thought may be subtle, not entirely conscious, but thoughts are identifiable. Beliefs are thoughts we have repeated to ourselves. We can identify a feeling or a thought or a belief in the moment. Depending upon our current subpersonality identification, our feelings or thoughts or beliefs shift.

In the Hero we are at our best, practicing release and gratitude and acceptance. In our Rebellious Teenager we don't own our power and we react impulsively. In our Defeated Child we no longer want the best for ourselves and we don't believe in ourselves.

Perhaps you identify with your Controller. We all have one. Your Controller may say, "Don't be stupid." Or "You've learned that lesson already." Or "Hurry up." What does your Controller communicate to you most frequently?

Maybe you practice a Needy Child vibration at times. You find yourself looking to others to change your sadness. You want to be rescued. Your hope lies outside yourself.

Perhaps you have noticed a Victimizer subpersonality. You like to poke others to see how they react. You deny your vulnerability and mock vulnerability in others.

We all have many subpersonalities, each practicing a different vibration. Let's know ourselves in terms of the vibrational frequencies we practice. Maybe in high anxiety situations you think and choose from your Competent Achiever. Maybe in relaxed times you identify with your Playful Child. Maybe your Efficient Administrator leads you through the work day.

Identify three of your subpersonalities and write about each one — how each thinks, what each believes, what their values are, and when you call upon them. These different energies live within you all the time. Notice the characteristic statements of each. Take some time now to write from three different subpersonalities you practice regularly.

(Completely separate from subpersonalities are multiple personalities. Research has shown that in one personality of a person diagnosed with Multiple Personality Disorder, the physical challenges are different from those in another personality. In the same body one personality may suffer from diabetes while another personality does not. Consciousness/vibratory practice is the only variant between one personality and another. Consciousness/vibratory practice affects health on every level.)

Notice your interactions last month. Does someone coax a certain vibration from you? Do you need to acknowledge that vibration in a different context? Maybe you have felt hurt by a slight from a stranger. In addition to forgiving him, whom else do you need to forgive? Do you need to forgive a subpersonality? Everything is connected. Nothing is random. Pay attention to the details of your life experience. Notice the depths inside to which they point.

Write about an interaction that mirrors a subpersonality relationship inside you. Notice the consistency of your experience, inside and outside.

When another is rude to us or acts unfairly, we focus on what we are being shown about ourselves. The vibration we encounter reflects a vibration already alive within us. We can only say Thank You when the Universe organizes encounters for our benefit. And everything benefits us. We need to look for the gift of increased clarity no matter what happens.

Increased clarity always supports us in receiving Source's unconditional love for us. What does a temporarily unpleasant situation matter if we open to Source a little more?

Chapter Twenty Five

You are a vibrational being. This is a vibrational Universe. Nothing stays as it is for more than a second unless we choose to hold on to it. Often we choose the same vibrational reality repeatedly, partly out of lack of awareness of what we do and partly out of an unwillingness to take complete responsibility for the life experience we create.

We notice one second at a time. We take responsibility for *what is* in the second and we choose again. We can repeat our choice or change our choice. No matter what we choose, the Universe says **Yes**. The Universe always respects our preference.

One way to avoid taking responsibility for what you create and, thus, for opening to Universal guidance is to debate the validity of these claims. As long as you reside in your head thinking, you don't practice the vulnerability which allows you to receive. That's why support groups where folks talk about their frustrations generally reinforce stuckness. When we agree about How-Life-Is we don't open to another experience of life.

Everything exists. Do you want to focus on your frustrations and limitations? You can if you want. They happened and continue to happen if you persist in focusing on them. Whatever you focus on will increase. Take responsibility for what you create.

Alternatively, you can focus on the reality currently emerging. Reality is vibrational before it manifests. What vibration are you practicing? That's the reality you will see around you.

The first manifestation of the new reality you choose comes through your feelings. You choose to practice the vibration and the feelings that accompany the reality you want to create. You feel the reality you choose before you see it. You manifest the reality you feel. Believing and feeling leads to seeing.

We need to be firmly anchored inside. We can't look to others to validate our pre-manifested reality. We don't need help and we don't need to convince anyone. We trust our guidance and refer to that truth inside us exclusively. We don't react to conditions around us or to good judgment or to realistic thinking. We know our chosen reality and that's all we know.

We appreciate the hints and nudges from the Universe which help us open more and more to receive unconditional love. Always they come. We trust our personal guidance. The Universe knows exactly what we need and always delivers the perfect opportunities for us to move forward. In our partnership with the Universe we pay attention and we trust our guidance. The Universe pays attention to us. Every second. In the second, the Universe knows if we betray our own best interests or if we honor them. Soon life brings us an experience to help us recognize our choice.

What amazing love and support! Never-ending, never-wavering. We need to pay attention.

Chapter Twenty Six

In our eternal center we feel pulled to expand. In this part of us we want to be all we can be. We choose to release limiting thoughts and we invite healing from a level we didn't create.

In our human center we prefer comfort, we want to fit in with others, and we resist dramatic shifts. Fear may influence our perspective and, without realizing it, we reduce our expectations.

The tension between our eternal center and our human center maintains. Consequences follow our choice to align with either center. Life always pulls us to integrate more of ourselves so that, often, comfort isn't possible. We cooperate with our expansion or we resist it.

Life experience has led us to a greater or lesser degree of trust for life. We maintain a momentum at a somewhat diminished level of consciousness in our effort to brook the divide between our two selves. In our eternal center we want to grow. In our human center we don't want to forge a path too different from our neighbors.

Rather than identify completely with either center we notice the relationship between the two. We notice when our thinking in our human center sabotages our expansion. We notice when our commitment to trust the Universe by meditating regularly disrupts our normal patterns of thought and makes functioning as we have known it impossible.

Receiving Source's unconditional love for us is not like opening presents on Christmas morning. Source doesn't indulge us. Source loves us and knows who we truly are. We have forgotten our eternal truth in our Essence but Source always pulls us there. Accepting Source's unconditional love requires us to loosen our identification with our human center.

This process of remembering our Essence bruises our pride. When we invite Source into the playground that is our consciousness, we watch what happens. We can't hold on to any corner of safety and comfort. We practice the surrender which is necessary to receive Source's unconditional love. So, we forego comfort and perceived safety and we say, "I am available and I trust completely."

We don't cling to anything from our human center that promises comfort. We accept new rules and different perspectives. We enter a world where we're not in charge and we commit to learn. No matter what happens we say, Thank You. We don't take offense. In this world we can't be disparaged or diminished for we don't take anything as other than what it is — Source's support for us being our best. And Source always supports us.

Source loves us overwhelmingly. Source doesn't settle for half measures. We never graduate and we never stop learning.

So many times I've witnessed folks jump into meditation only to back off a few weeks later when their life experience changes unpredictably. They lose their comfort when they meet feelings long buried and flee back into their human center thinking. What would get them through this disruptive time is staying in their eternal center and continuing to be available for healing. Acceptance of vulnerability at a deeper level is required. This scares many folks who would prefer to close that door and think rather than feel and practice surrender.

Trusting Source day in and day out regardless of what we feel or what happens to us rocks us to our core which actually is the definition of allowing Source to work in our lives. We don't hold on to anything but our attitude of surrender and our trust. We know that Source loves us. We allow ourselves to receive that love by not focusing on conditions but by knowing the truth which is that we are expressions of Source Energy. Regardless of what we feel or what happens to us, that statement stands.

Living as expressions of Source Energy implies that we honor our experience as sacred. We don't compare ourselves to others and we never judge ourselves. We notice and we wonder and we learn, respecting the ineffable quality of our experience. We're not impressed with ourselves or boastful but we are humbly aware that Source lives through us. We want to pay attention to both our inner world and the outer world and learn. Consciousness is our playground. By noticing our experience from our detached Observer we learn the specifics of our thinking that lead to particular interactions with others. How we treat ourselves is reflected to us by others who treat us the way we treat ourselves. There's no need for affront. What we see outside us shows us what we refuse to see inside. By increasing our awareness of our subtle dynamics we grow.

The resonance between our human and our eternal centers determines our life experience. Usually changing our experience is more a matter of being than doing. Deciding is more powerful than efforting. Our consciousness forms the basis for our experience. And working with our consciousness is the fastest way to change our experience.

Manifestations result from our vibrational practice. But we realize that manifestations are inconsequential. With a solid vibrational practice we learn that we can manifest what we want, maybe not immediately but eventually. Our daily aligned vibrational practice assumes primary importance. We experience oneness with Source consciously and that confirms and makes meaningful our experience. There are no accidents. We can appreciate the truth of even the most mundane aspects of our experience if we focus.

Chapter Twenty Seven

I received a gift from Source this weekend of the icky variety. My friend Jan and I dined at a middle Eastern restaurant. Jan is a loving, accepting friend who has been super-supportive. At the restaurant she ordered one of her favorite dishes which we split — homemade potato chips with onions and garlic. I was delirious with appreciation. I ate and ate and ate until not a crumb remained. I can't remember when I've enjoyed food so much.

The waiter smirked (judgmentally, I thought, but who knows). Suddenly, I felt embarrassed by my enthusiasm. When I climbed in bed I felt a non-physical heaviness, the familiar Controller anger. I felt it when I awoke during the night and it was present the next day. The intensity of my Controller's judgment and anger and abuse brought me to tears. I felt labeled not OK, lacking, stupid, inappropriate, and vulnerable. I wanted to apologize to this non-physical entity and promise to do better. I recognized the Unwanted Child trying to retrieve lost favor. Shame consumed me.

The following day the feelings lingered. At the 7am meditation group I noticed the Child's shame, the sense of unworthiness, and the longing. But I also noticed anger that I was treated abusively by this ephemeral Controller. I've learned to watch the Controller behind the Observer window. Her attacks mask her pain. I want to see the pain, not get distracted by her hostility.

Later in the day I received an abusive email message. I recognized the reflection of my inner world abuse. But I also felt my anger. I blocked the emails and committed to my Child that I love her and I will always protect her. I don't care how she acts or what others think of her. I adore her and I always will. I will never expect her to rein herself in and be perfect and look for approval from others. I am the Parent and her Supporter and her Protector. I am on her side no matter what.

The next day I felt guided to submit an article to a magazine I haven't approached before. I knew this was a publishable article but my attempts to contact the magazines I usually work with were all thwarted in unusual ways. When the submission proceeded so easily I saw Source's aid in making it happen. I did my inner work and allowed healing of an old pain and the outer world responded immediately.

Tonight I notice that my shoulders relax. I feel like I can present myself to the world, shoulders back, upright posture, and announce that I'm not perfect and I'm not trying to be but I'm here. And I'm worthy of notice. And I'm fine right now this minute just the way I am.

Joy derives from our attitudes of trust and allowing, not from conditions. In our opening to receive Source's love, we don't react to anything or anyone. We focus on our vibrational alignment. That's all we care about. Walking through life in partnership with Source makes our days sparkle. And those days that challenge us bring gifts of increasing clarity. We never doubt our partnership or our worthiness.

Chapter Twenty Eight

My guidance is specific and momentary. I do my work by paying attention to my inner world tugs. Any intellectual component follows the emotional release and the attitude of allowing. Healing is completely personal.

We each have our own challenges. My lifelong inner world antipathy between my Controller and my Child (my thinking and my feeling) may not resemble your status quo. You map the dynamics of your own inner world process. This element is essential, not in the intellectualizing of the healing process but in the acceptance of it being completely personal and, to a large degree, solitary. Timing is personal. I can't criticize myself for still feeling old hurts but I can always commit to practicing presence and allowing and noticing *what is* this second.

Source doesn't judge us or criticize us. When we judge or criticize (ourselves or another), we cut ourselves off from Source. Usually behind judgment and criticism is our unwillingness to be present to our vulnerability. **Source works in us through our vulnerability**. When we refuse to experience our own vulnerability we disallow Source. We resist experiencing our vulnerability by talking about it or thinking about it or objectifying it. ("I'm a member of this group and we always say . . .")

It doesn't matter where psychically we stand this second. All that matters is our willingness to allow Source to heal us. We can't think of ourselves as already complete or as unworthy. We simply are, this second, and we respect ourselves. Detachment supports us in this attitude which precedes movement. Accepting the present moment allows us to experience it, to release it, and to welcome the next.

Chapter Twenty Nine

Acceptance is a powerful spiritual practice. When we accept, we say Yes to *what is* and, thereby, acknowledge that we are ready to learn. This lifetime is a school room. We notice what we like and what we don't. We practice being less or more of ourselves. We notice interactions with others and different ways of responding. We learn to know ourselves as we have been, as we are now, and as we are becoming.

We are always becoming. We may not always be performing an action but becoming implies evolution and growth on inner levels. **The first step in growth is acceptance of this second.**

We don't have to like *what is* but we do have to accept *what is* if we choose to grow. We practice presence in this second and we acknowledge that this second is perfect. Perfect for us to see where we are emotionally. Perfect for us to notice the degree of self-acceptance we practice. Perfect for us to notice the acceptance we practice for others.

What we don't accept in ourselves, we don't accept in others. When we practice gentleness with ourselves, we practice gentleness with others. When we hate our vulnerability, we hate vulnerability in others. (It's always interesting to notice who annoys you and what vibration they practice. They are fine, just the way they are this second. Your reaction tells you something about yourself.) We are never so evolved that we point fingers or judge. We notice our Controller but we don't identify with it in relationships.

Acceptance does not imply agreement. We may or may not like *what is* but our acceptance of this second just the way it is allows the next step to present itself. When we accept *what is, what is* changes. When we rail against *what is*, nothing changes. Are we cooperating in our own growth or resisting growth? Are we humble, allowing ourselves to be guided? Are we identified with the ever-flowing, ever-changing being that we basically are or do we enjoy the structure of our roles?

We notice. We're not trying to fit an image. We're discovering who we are and what our gifts are. We allow ourselves to be carried by the flow. And we appreciate it, whether or not we understand it. Whether or not we like it. Always we appreciate the healing flow that is our life experience.

Acceptance may seem like a minimal or a major challenge. All we do is say Thank You for *whatever is* right now. We don't evaluate or critique. Just Thank You.

Acceptance of our feelings may be challenging. We don't choose our feelings consciously. We may judge them or disparage them or deny them. But most basically we choose to practice acceptance of our feelings regardless of what they are. Rage, horror, fear, sadness — they all carry a vibrational frequency. We stay behind the Observer window, we practice presence, and we notice whatever vibrational frequency we practice.

Practicing acceptance releases resistance; this is the primary value of practicing acceptance. It's not about <u>what</u> we accept. It's about the process of not resisting anything. With acceptance we find peace in the moment and we allow.

Practicing acceptance is an easy way to align with Source Energy. Acceptance reduces the tension between our human and our eternal centers. It moves us into our identification with our Essence. And in our Essence we are carried to healing. With acceptance we erase the labels of "problem" and "unwanted." With acceptance we notice *what is*. That's all. We don't struggle or judge or resist. We simply accept this second just the way it is and we practice presence. A valuable skill for every human.

Chapter Thirty

My dream image upon awakening: a small group including me crouches on the floor talking in subdued tones. The sun shines brilliantly through the sheer blinds. A person outside the building walks around and around looking for us. We want to avoid him but we don't fear him. He's annoying but he's not dangerous.

Initially in the dream I squat in a less than powerful position. To make the dream turn out well, I can stand up, move into my Spiritual Warrior, and speak to the person outside, telling him what I want.

That action of standing tall, moving into my Spiritual Warrior, and speaking my truth offers me valuable guidance in many situations. I think of speaking with the abusive Controller whom earlier this week I encountered both within me and outside me. That figure has loomed prominently all my life, fostering depression and alienation from myself and from others. Now my dream tells me I can positively influence this inner world relationship. This is an insight of transformative proportions. Nothing could improve the quality of my life more than ending this internal war.

Adult: Welcome. Come inside and let's talk.

Controller: I've been looking for you. You need to listen to me.

Adult: I do need to speak with you but I need you to listen.

Controller: You'd better pay attention to me or you will mess up, maybe publicly. You could embarrass yourself so much that you won't be comfortable in the world at all. I'm your only hope.

Adult: Actually, you are not but I understand that you think so. You never talk about the fear behind your demands. Why don't you tell me about your fear?

Controller: I'm afraid of not making it in the world. I fear being judged unacceptable. I fear appearing graceless. I fear being hated. I fear dying from lack of support.

Adult: Those are huge fears and terribly painful. I know you've lived with them for decades. The intensity of your fears amazes me.

Controller: I can't let them overwhelm me. I will keep them at bay by not making mistakes and by not acting stupid. I don't expect gentleness. I can make it on my own.

Adult: You have done a great job of surviving. I give you that. I know you haven't been happy.

Controller: I don't expect to be happy. I just need to survive.

Adult: You don't even hope for more, do you?

Controller: How many times do I have the same experience before I recognize the pattern?

Adult: Change comes now. I can feel it. We can heal this split.

Controller: I don't do healing. I survive in the face of danger.

Accepting Unconditional Love

Adult: Yes, I get that. I will invite and allow healing. I know that scares you. It's a totally different world and I'm not sure you can enter it. But I will take it from here.

Controller: Think about what you are doing.

Adult: I probably won't think. I'll trust the Universe and open to healing.

Controller: I don't know what you mean. Just don't be stupid.

Adult: I probably will look stupid sometimes. I'll risk that.

Controller: Not such good judgment. Try to stay in control.

Adult: No, I won't try to stay in control. That part of my life is over. I'm going for aliveness and passion and transcendence now.

Controller: Listen to me. You are not safe.

Adult: I know you think that and you live by that premise. I choose to live from the assumption that I will be protected and guided.

Controller: Don't be naive. You've seen folks in the world be rude to you.

Adult: And I've seen how they reflect me to myself. They actually reflect you to me. I understand you're anchored in fear but your words to me have been so abusive. That's ending now. I used to hate you for your abuse but now I see that you can't be otherwise. I also see that I need to parent you. I won't accept your abusive words but I will show you another way to act.

You really are a small child who needs to be nurtured and allowed to mature. I know you are not available to receive kindness.

I see you and I know your pain. I know that you don't want to feel it. I feel it and I feel your abuse inside me and once in a while from outside me. I know you are hurting and I know you won't accept that truth.

You are my responsibility and I will know your truth even if you don't want to be known. You are hurting and you are afraid and, I dare say, you are overwhelmed by worldly expectations. I know you are basically good. I know at your core a beautiful light shines. I also know that scares you and you prefer to avoid your inner world. But I know you and I see your sadness and I will hold you as you heal. I won't take your abuse personally and I won't react. I know you in your highest and your best healed self. And I know this Controller role is just for protection because you don't know that healing is possible. I will know healing for both of us. I will allow healing and I won't let you sabotage it.

That Controller presents as an overgrown Problem Child who disrupts my life. OK, a child is a child. I'll love her instead of viewing her as a Parent and wanting her to love me. She can be a problem but mostly she is a damaged child. I'm not intimidated and I won't withdraw from her.

Reflections of her in the world are another story, however. When I encounter abuse I won't understand or be patient. I'll excuse myself and not let it happen a second time. There are abusers in the world and I want to recognize them. I'm not available for anyone's abuse. I won't be abusive myself but I do need to keep firm boundaries. That means not looking outside myself for what I need. I'm glad that I own my vulnerability but I'll shield myself from abusive others who don't value vulnerability. I'll stay in my Adult inside me with the Controllers in the world. I won't make anyone wrong but I will always protect myself. And always I will see behind my own Controller's abusive facade and help her to heal. That's my job.

Chapter Thirty One

We live one moment at a time. We practice acceptance and presence in the moment. We trust and we allow because we know we are guided. We don't know how we are guided but we know that Source always wants more for us than we can imagine for ourselves.

We're not proprietary about our life experience. We say Yes to recognizing very part of us. Who we are is greater than who we think we are. We practice humility in the face of that truth. We're humble about moving through our days, always keeping an ear attuned to our guidance. Any second could be the setting for a miracle and we don't want to miss an opportunity for a miracle.

What if Source wants to give us a huge gift? We'd better pay attention and be ready to receive! And if we are attentive and open to receiving, there's a good chance a gift will come to us.

Reality isn't predetermined. We choose our openness and our receptivity and that influences what comes to us. Of course, this isn't a matter of saying affirmations but of meaning affirmations. The Universe knows what you mean regardless of what you say.

How can we practice openness to receive a miracle? First we practice peace inside. We allow our subpersonality conflicts to heal. We move into our Observer and watch the Universe work in our life, inner and outer. And we do that often. We show up, we pay attention, and we allow. What could be simpler?

Avoiding our vulnerability might feel simpler. Intellectualizing instead of allowing may feel simpler. Keeping on the move instead of practicing presence seems much simpler.

But let's assume you are past these questions. You meditate daily. You practice presence. You pay attention. And the more you do so, the more your experience shifts in unpredictable ways. You trust enough to accept that and to allow. You notice *what is* inside you and you allow healing. You know that your healing is a sacred process and you appreciate that process. You accept and allow and notice and accept and allow and notice. You stay in the present second, practicing forgiveness and gratitude. And?

And what? That is the question. You live your life as an ever-evolving experience, not as a series of goals achieved. You experience your aliveness in seconds. You notice your decisions and their consequences. You see corollaries inside and outside you. Details carry meaning.

You experience your partnership with Source and you trust it. You lose more anxiety all the time. You trust your feelings and express them appropriately in the moment. You are not threatened by others nor do you need anything from them.

Life becomes fun and meaningful.

But you want a miracle. How do you invite a miracle? You know you can't force it yourself. You can't even think it into reality. You can imagine it already here and feel what that feels like.

Miracles are yours. You have to know that and to expect that. Nothing is too huge for Source. When you practice alignment with Source, you know what Source knows, at least in the second. You know perfect health and financial well-being and joy-filled relationships. You know you are unlimited in your Essence in your eternal center. And that's really where you enjoy hanging out.

In your Essence in your eternal center, you are the most you you can be. You are unique. You know your value and you accept it. You dream. Big.

What is an unrealistic dream that you truly want? Can you see yourself experiencing it in this second? How does that feel? Practice that vibration.

If you can't imagine it, look at the belief that keeps you from receiving your highest good. You are the only one who limits yourself. Notice how you do that. If you want to change that limiting vibration, you can. This second.

Do you want to let go of your limited thinking and your fear of your feelings? Do you want to move out of your comfortable box and experience life on a plane you haven't known? How much aliveness do you want? It's up to you.

The Universe delivers miracles when we release our resistance.

Chapter Thirty Two

"Fierce" seems to be the word for the day, possibly for every day the rest of my life. It has been clear for many weeks that I cannot progress by my Controller taking action. Two days ago I walked to the corner and back, .4 of a mile. The winter sun warmed the breeze. I wasn't pushing to see how far I could walk. I enjoyed the time outside.

The fatigue resulting from the walk confined me to resting until bed time. I felt discouraged and confused. I had checked with my Controller before I set out to confirm that I wasn't indulging that part of me. But clearly my Controller operates so subtly that I don't notice it.

I realized in my meditation this morning that I am called to practice a deeper level of surrender. It's not about releasing my dreams and hopes for perfect walking. I still see that coming. But I am completely perplexed about how that will occur. Not through exercise or good habits or affirmations. Not from using good judgment. No Controller input, no trying, no good ideas will be tolerated. Now I am thrown into an arena where only a miracle can take me where I want to go.

OK. I'm ready for a miracle, as the song says. And welcoming and completely trusting. I know a miracle comes to me now.

I had expected the cessation of my daily swims a few months ago to leave me disgruntled. Quite the opposite happened. I enjoyed not arising at 4:30. The day seemed so much easier without the early morning flurry of activity.

Now I am shown that I can't hold on to anything except my knowing that I am being healed. I must <u>allow</u> healing. I can't force it or even help it. I can only receive healing. So I need to maintain a perpetual state of openness and receptivity.

I have given myself some gifts recently. I've wanted some new art. Instead of bargaining with myself to buy it after achieving a goal, I gave it to myself now. That act and that attitude propel me into a realm of receiving and celebrating. (One print is entitled Celebration.) And, really, isn't that where I want to live? Always receiving and always celebrating and always inviting miracles.

Perfect walking at this point looks to me like it requires a miracle. But that's OK. I know I'm blessed with unlimited miracles. I allow miracles.

I surrender to the Universe. Clearly, I can't <u>do</u> anything to effect my healing. I need to start the day with trust that even if I haven't slept well, I will be supported in functioning well. Even if I'm not aware of the details of what's asked of me, I can trust that I will be fine. That invites the Universe to operate with greater scope in my life. Or rather, that alerts me to notice that the Universe already operates in the details of my life.

More and more I see that I can't live my life satisfactorily relying only upon my own resources. Source reassures me that I will be taken care of in ways I can't predict or even necessarily see. What could be better? What deserves celebration more than receiving Source's reassurance?

Practicing passivity with an attitude of fierceness solidifies my commitment to allow the Universe to guide me. And It's telling me that It will. I have no doubts or concerns. I will enjoy noticing each step in this healing journey.

Chapter Thirty Three

Everything is consciousness. The more I allow in meditation the more healing I notice in every part of my life. My right leg feels more normal and more connected to the ground than it has in years. I no longer pull it along but I can swing it ahead of me. That feels like confidence, like I own my existence here on earth. I have a right to be. I feel confirmed in being myself today just the way I am.

These words sound naive but I'm experiencing them at a level I haven't visited before. When I see the vast influence of my consciousness I am humbled. When I see how tiny details influence the whole of my life's experience I feel humbled even more. I notice how I erect and distort my experience of myself and the world by seeing without clarity. I distort the clarity in my perceptions by not allowing the flow. And I disallow the flow by turning away from feeling my feelings.

That happens subtly and instantaneously. Source is aware of my consciousness in the second and my distortions of consciousness in the same second. In my intellect I am not that clear.

A month ago I put out the heavy recycling bin on trash day. A gentle rain had dampened the sidewalk and the bin lurched away from me, dragging me to the sidewalk. My glasses were destroyed and blood covered my face. Reflecting upon my consciousness at that moment I realized that I had chosen to ignore my feelings and move into my Controller's taking-care-of-business attitude. The fall jerked me back to paying attention to my inner world in the moment.

What a wonderfully precise intervention! Source notices every tiny detail of my pulling myself out of the flow. And lets me know, too. The scrapes on my face taught me not to ignore my feelings. It was such a hard fall with such intense consequences for me in terms of blood and my glasses being destroyed that it focused my attention. A message I won't forget. A choice I won't repeat.

When I didn't wear my glasses I realized that I don't need them. My vision is better without them. I had prayed for improved vision. My prayer was answered and in this dramatic way I acknowledged it. A couple weeks healed my facial scrapes but I retained the lesson that my consciousness in every second counts. And Source knows everything immediately.

Source knows my every tenth-of-a-second vibrational practice. That practice affects every part of my life. Like pulling a string in a fabric, every subtle thought and reaction affects the whole of my experience. I can't heal physically if I'm not integrating my healed vibrational practice into the whole of who I am.

I can't cut off any part of myself and hope to heal. If I don't accept my angry feelings and value them and integrate them by noticing what lies behind them, I won't be able to walk well. And I can't very well ask for more to be given to me if I refuse to accept what does come. I can't be in my Controller making judgments about my experience (not wanting to feel) and allow Source to work in my life. And, really, it is all about allowing.

I acknowledge that Source knows best. I accept that Source wants my healing more than I do. I trust that Source knows what experiences I need to progress in my healing. I realize that at the right moment Source provides exactly the experience I need in order to move toward my full healing. Put it that way and it sounds simple. Which it is. It requires only my paying attention in the second and allowing Source and noticing how I'm led. I'm reassured that I can trust a wisdom greater than my mind's.

So, accepting that Source wants my complete healing, I employ an attitude of curiosity and respect in response to my day's experiences. I know that Source wants to give me a miracle. First

I need to believe that. Then I need to not block it. Then I need to accept and celebrate it. I need to trust that a miracle comes and to allow it rather than evaluate it. I prepare the soil to accept unconditional love by not thinking. I reside in my heart and I allow and, thus, I live in the flow.

Sometimes when I guide a meditation I say, "'No matter what exists this second, we say Yes." That's it. Always Yes. Always I trust Source completely. Always I am available. Always Yes. Why wouldn't we live with that acceptance of every second of every day?

I think it's not because we fear Source but because we fear some part of ourselves. Most of us nurture such incredible disdain for ourselves. How can we even contemplate Source loving us? We certainly don't love ourselves. And if Source truly knew us It wouldn't love us, either. Except Source knows us better than we know ourselves and Source adores us. We can't make sense of that fact. And certainly we can't believe it or truly accept it. Source adores me? You've got to be kidding. Certainly, Source has better taste than that.

It's so much easier to push away Source's love than it is to accept it. I believe that we don't want to be unconditionally loved by Source. What guilt that invites! What, me? Accepting unconditional love? Does Source really know my ugly thoughts? Actually, yes, Source does. And Source loves me anyway? We don't let our friends or even our mates know the dastardly mental scenarios that dot our inner world landscapes. We fear they'd abandon us in a second if they glimpsed that dirt. But Source knows every tiny hate and revulsion and distortion and still adores us.

It doesn't make sense. We readily agree that we don't deserve to be adored for any of twelve reasons which we spout without hesitation. But the rock bottom foundational fact is that Source adores us. We haven't earned that unconditional love. We don't think we deserve it. We'd rather push it away than accept it. And still Source loves us unconditionally. We can't change that.

I hear so many folks talk about their disreputable deeds from decades ago. They harbor shame. They say they forgive themselves but clearly their hearts aren't open to receive. They can't punish themselves enough to finally be OK. Their Controllers grip their collars and swing them around and nothing changes. Perpetually guilty, perpetually lacking, perpetually disappointed.

We cringe when we think of a child we love not liking himself. But we abuse ourselves chronically and we feel OK about it. When we stop and think about it, we decide to continue abusing ourselves. After all, our Controller rationalizes, we deserve it. We remember those incidents forty years ago and we use them to beat ourselves up today. Or we may say, "It's my Critic who hates me. I'm just the Victim."

It's time we grow up. Prolonging that childhood dynamic paralyzes us. We all wish we had made better choices about something. That's why we're here — to learn and to grow. If we do everything perfectly, why experience life? I imagine that before we incarnate, we feel eager and optimistic about coming to this plane. We're open to experiencing our feelings. We expect to learn.

When do we lose our enthusiasm for living and close down on our aliveness? When do we choose to deaden our insides and pretend that's acceptable? When do we lose confidence in Source? When do we forget that we are expressions of Source Energy? When do we choose to live without accepting or expecting love? How do we abandon ourselves? And why, when life disappoints us, do we abandon ourselves? Why is self-hatred so much easier than self-acceptance?

Accepting love takes work. We have to shake away those binding ropes that reduce our aliveness. We trust another and let ourselves be known in our vulnerability. More or less.

Accepting unconditional love requires a radical restructuring of our self-awareness. We can't focus primarily on our self-described deficits. We must acknowledge our oneness with Source. That's nothing to be proud of or ashamed of. Simply acknowledging it shakes our foundation. **How can we continue to live our lives in the ordinary way knowing clearly that we are one with Source?**

Our awareness of our oneness with Source leads us to release our sabotaging attitudes. We let them go because we need to, not because we feel like it. We stop tolerating the stance that keeps us small. We choose to experience our oneness with Source and we release anything in us that inhibits that. It's our choice. And we make it every day. By choosing wholeness we reclaim our souls.

PART TWO

Accepting unconditional love is a way of living, not a behavior. In Part Two you practice accepting unconditional love in the context of your daily experience. Open to any page. The suggestions focus your attention. Keep the perspective with you as you move through your day. Notice your experience.

You can practice these exercises repeatedly over the years. Always you will move more deeply inside, exploring your current level of consciousness. Always you will be guided.

Accepting Unconditional Love

Today know that at your deepest center, Source lives. You are an expression of Source Energy.

Today notice how life responds to your unvoiced thoughts and feelings.

Accepting Unconditional Love

Today notice when you let yourself experience your feelings and when you don't. Notice the beliefs behind not allowing yourself to feel your feelings.

Today allow whatever feelings live in you to be, just as they are. Pay attention to your inner world experience and observe.

Today notice how your outer world encounters reflect your inner world.

Notice when you are comfortable with yourself and when you are uncomfortable with yourself. Let yourself experience each. Stay in your Observer.

Accepting Unconditional Love

Today don't criticize yourself or anyone else. Practice appreciation.

Ruth Cherry, Ph.D.

Today appreciate your vulnerability and your sensitivity.

Accepting Unconditional Love

Today notice your thoughts without thinking your thoughts.

Today acknowledge your feelings without identifying with your feelings.

Notice your thoughts and your feelings moving through you without labeling them "mine." Don't hold on to them. Watch them pass.

Today remember the You that lives at your eternal center, deeper than your thoughts and your feelings.

Practicing presence means noticing *what is* each second from your detached Observer. Today practice presence for a few minutes three times.

I encourage you to want, not to settle, not to be realistic. Today know what you want, see it come into being, know it real.

Today notice when you stay on your own side and when you abandon yourself. You can always choose again to be on your own side.

Today practice receiving. Receiving requires that you maintain a respectful stance toward your vulnerability as you move through the day.

Accepting Unconditional Love

Today choose awareness of *what is* rather than choosing comfort.

Today practice humility. Say Thank You for whatever happens.

Accepting Unconditional Love

Throughout the day ask yourself, What vibration am I practicing this second?

Today notice when you jump out of the present vibrational moment into the past or the future.

Accepting Unconditional Love

Just for today let go of worry.

Today know that you are worthy. Be aware of your worthiness all day.

Accepting Unconditional Love

What old unnecessary thoughts grip you and hold on? Today release them. If they come up again, turn away and practice appreciation for something else.

Today accept responsibility for whatever happens to you.

Accepting Unconditional Love

Today you will be given gifts. Pay attention.

Today acknowledge the unconditional love that already lives at your core. It's available to you every second.

Accepting Unconditional Love

Just for today, don't play it safe.

Whatever you want to experience on your very best day in the future, practice feeling that today.

Today dance with Source.

Today notice when your thoughts diminish your experience and when they enhance it.

When you notice self-sabotaging thoughts, let them go and choose affirming self-talk.

A power greater than your own flows to you and through you. Be aware of that today and celebrate it.

Accepting Unconditional Love

Today choose not to take offense. Appreciate whatever is.

No matter what happens today, stay on your own side. Treat yourself respectfully and gently.

Accepting Unconditional Love

Today notice what you pay attention to. You can change your focus at any moment.

Let today be a day you grow in appreciation for yourself.

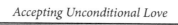

Today cooperate with life. Don't fight your experience.

Live today with passion, saying Yes to whatever is in front of you.

Accepting Unconditional Love

Source believes in you and wants the best for you. Remember that today.

Acceptance is trusting life more than you trust your intellect. Today practice acceptance.

Accepting Unconditional Love

Notice how your encounters with others reflect your inner world vibrational practice.

Since the Universe is still creating itself, you being fully you contributes to the whole. Today know that you are valuable.

Accepting Unconditional Love

Today believe in yourself.

Release one limiting mistaken belief about yourself today. Replace it with one appreciative thought.

Today practice respect for yourself as a unique expression of Source Energy.

Ruth Cherry, Ph.D.

Today trust your intuition.

Accepting Unconditional Love

In one part of your consciousness, you feel powerless. In another part you feel empowered. Notice which part of your consciousness you practice today. You can change your vibrational practice any second you want.

At one point today choose to be available to Source. Be still for five minutes and let your in-breath carry your attention into your deepest eternal center.

Accepting Unconditional Love

No matter what happens today ask yourself, What am I being shown about myself? How is this an opportunity for my growth?

Source pays attention to you every second. Remember that today.

Accepting Unconditional Love

Today invite magic to work in your life.

Notice giant garden shears cutting any unnecessary ties to the past. See that image all day.

Accepting Unconditional Love

Today practice not reacting to conditions around you. Stay anchored in your eternal center no matter what happens.

Today notice how the Universe supports you in doing your inner work.

Accepting Unconditional Love

Whom do you need to forgive? Which of your inner world subpersonalities does that person reflect to you? Today appreciate that person. And that subpersonality.

Practicing presence invites feelings that need to be healed to arise. Today practice presence and allow.

Accepting Unconditional Love

Today trust that your healing proceeds even though your intellect may not understand it.

Ruth Cherry, Ph.D.

Today play with the Universe. Ask and observe.

Accepting Unconditional Love

Today practice trusting the Universe in any way you choose.

Ruth Cherry, Ph.D.

Today ask the Universe for help in a specific situation.

Accepting Unconditional Love

Today reconsider one of your assumptions about what you cannot do.

Today practice gratitude for what is in your life that you don't want. Remember that it is a gift. Don't resist it.

Accepting Unconditional Love

Today welcome a part of you that you don't usually welcome.

Today catch yourself when you are resisting life — when you criticize others, when you avoid your feelings, when your thoughts lead you away from joy. Then choose again.

Today practice availability to Source by not thinking. Focus on experiencing the present moment.

Play with nature today and notice how nature plays with you.

Accepting Unconditional Love

When something unexpected or unsettling happens today, know that you are experiencing Source's unconditional love for you. Look for the gift.

Practice stillness for twenty seconds twice today.

Accepting Unconditional Love

Today choose the vibration you want to practice. Reset your practice throughout the day if you lose your focus.

Today ignore conditions. Focus on the emerging reality you are creating, not on the one you observe.

Accepting Unconditional Love

Notice Source operating in your life today.

CPSIA information can be obtained
at www.ICGtesting.com
Printed in the USA
BVHW070624291221
625049BV00002B/379